Leading Global Project Teams

The New Leadership Challenge

Russ J. Martinelli
Tim J. Rahschulte
James M. Waddell

First Edition

Multi-Media
P u b l i c a t i o n s Inc.
Oshawa, Ontario, Canada

Leading Global Project Teams: The New Leadership Challenge
by Russ J. Martinelli, Tim J. Rahschulte, and James M. Waddell

Managing Editor: Kevin Aguanno
Typesetting: Charles Sin
Cover Design: Troy O'Brien
eBook Converstion: Agustina Baid

Published by:
Multi-Media Publications Inc.
Box 58043, Rosslynn RPO
Oshawa, ON, Canada, L1J 8L6

http://www.mmpubs.com/

Paperback   ISBN-10: 155489064X   ISBN-13: 9781554890644
Adobe PDF ebook   ISBN-10: 1554890756   ISBN-13: 9781554890750

Published in Canada. Printed simultaneously in the United States and the United Kingdom.

CIP data available from the publisher.

Table of Contents

3

Wdedicate this book to our families who keep us grounded and focused on what's important, and to our circle of globally distributed friends who remind us how blessed we are.

Russ J. Martinelli
Tim J. Rahschulte
James M. Waddell

Preface

At first, globalization may be perceived as something "out there" that is not applicable to your business let alone you or your life. What comes to mind when the word globalization is used in your conversations? It may conjure up ideas of off-shoring work from one country to another for the promise of business process efficiencies and lower cost to produce goods and services. Certainly, in North America, off-shoring of work over the past several decades has fueled a heated debate over whether globalization is good or bad for the country. The term globalization may also bring to mind the seemingly bureaucratic and quasi-governmental organizations like the World Trade Organization, International Monetary Fund, or World Bank. Each of which has a charter to increase global trade and monetary exchange.

Globalization is more than simply off-shoring work or establishing government programs aimed at expanding trade. Pressures from emerging markets, converging markets, technology advances, customer demands, product sourcing options, and resource availability have stimulated globalization as a means to improve business results. Undeniably, our globe is quickly becoming a smaller, flatter, and a more level playing field on which to compete; however, small, flat, and level are not synonyms for *easy* or *effective.*

The strategy to improve business results through globalization has become increasingly common. Success in reaping the business value intended from a globalization strategy is, unfortunately, not as common. As our national boundaries blur and we grow more connected through global collaboration, the dynamics of organizational life grow more complex. These complexities offer challenge, confusion, and frustration – but also great opportunity! The key to achieving improved business results does not hinge on strategies alone, but also in our ability to effectively lead global product and service development teams to successfully execute the strategies. Our research and experience show that those struggling the most are the practitioners who find their historic team leadership practices ineffective in today's global business model. It is the challenges of these people that we address in this book.

Specifically, we answer the question: "How does one effectively lead global, highly distributed teams to achieve the improved business results needed to compete in today's market?"

This book answers that question and more. In short, it is not the work of just one leader that delivers business results, but of many working as a collective, collaborative team that happens to be separated by distance, time, and culture; therefore, we address the new leadership challenge of leading a globally distributed organization by focusing on the responsibilities of the collective team – from senior managers to individuals that make up our global project teams.

To effectively lead a global team, one must first understand the forces driving our companies to a global business model. The first part of this book, Chapters One through Three, offer an explanation as to why organizations globalize, along with the barriers and challenges encountered by most when global execution fails to achieve globalization goals. Illustrated case studies support the need for foundational elements necessary for success in a global business model. While largely the role of senior leaders, this section details the criticality of creating a firm foundation to support their people leading global teams.

We then delve into the 'how-to' of effective global team leadership. The team leadership concepts offered are not new, and have already been proven effective for leading non-global teams. What is new is the knowledge provided on how to refocus and expand these concepts for use in a global team environment. Leveraging practical case studies and interviews with global team leaders from best practice companies in Chapters Four through Six, this section highlights the roles, responsibilities, duties, and actions necessary to create and sustain an effective team that is distributed across the globe.

Knowing most organizations are still in search of greater effectiveness in global team leadership, Chapters Seven and Eight addresses the organizational transition necessary to effectively globalize your teams and business. Starting with the foundational elements outlined in the beginning chapters, coupled with the effective team leadership concepts, this last section offers a transitional change management framework for realization of improved business results through effective global product and service development.

The ongoing search for greater organizational efficiency and effectiveness is being addressed through resourcing business needs around the globe – to those most appropriately positioned and resourced to optimize business operations and meet customer needs. Realizing such effectiveness and efficiency is challenging to say the least. Based on our global experience and data from our research, it is one of the most pressing new leadership challenges of our day. To make the situation worse is that leading global teams is not an inherent trait or skill set. The silver lining is that effectively leading global teams can be a learned skill.

This book is aimed to help understand the challenges of global teams and, perhaps even more importantly, offer educational value in terms of how one can learn to bring organizational effectiveness into alignment with the continually changing global business environment.

CHAPTER ONE

Going Global

"I believe in looking reality straight in the eye and denying it."
- Garrison Keilor

As Scott Jones hung up the phone, the reality of his situation began to set in – there are globalization leaders and there are globalization followers, and he was working for a globalization follower. Both he and the company he works for are feeling the pressure to rapidly catch up competitively to the globalization leaders within their industry.

Several months prior, Jones was offered and had accepted the Director of New Product Development position with a company in the consumer electronics industry named Keytron. Although he was not looking to change employers, he felt his career had reached a plateau, and a new challenge would be welcomed if the right opportunity presented itself. At the time, the position at Keytron seemed to be that right opportunity. Now, however, he was not so sure.

Even though Keytron is not one of the top enterprises in the consumer electronics industry, they have grown at a consistent and healthy rate and have plans to continue increasing their market presence. Primarily through a strategy of mergers and acquisitions, they are positioned to be one of the world's top five consumer electronics companies within the next five to seven years. As Director of New Product Development, Jones sees that he will be at the heart of the company's engine of growth as they create innovative products for new and expanding markets.

However, this is a very different and more complex environment than what Jones has experienced to date. As a result of the mergers and acquisitions strategy, new product development at Keytron is now distributed across several countries and continents. Product design is performed at five sites – two in Europe, two in the United States, and one in India. Additionally, product integration and testing occurs in Mexico, final production is in the process of being transferred from the United States to China, and a major component for many of Keytron's products is designed and manufactured by a strategic alliance partner in Korea. Jones' new product development teams are now highly distributed across the globe and thus face many more challenges than Jones originally envisioned.

As the person responsible for improving Keytron's development performance in a highly distributed and global environment, Jones realized he was in a predicament. This highly distributed model is entirely new to him. New product development at his previous employer was performed at a single site in the United States and the new product development teams were co-located and highly integrated. Because of this, he lacks the direct experience in leading highly distributed global teams from which to draw upon and use in his new role. Like any good senior leader, however, he began looking to his network of people who he knew possessed the direct experience in leading global teams for advice, guidance, and support.

Jones decided to first contact one of his industry colleagues who has experience working for a large multi-national company.

Like Jones, Melissa Doyle was a new product development director and worked for a leading manufacturer in the high-tech industry. As Jones and Doyle began their conversation, Jones explained that he had taken a new position since they met last, and was contacting Doyle in hopes of gaining some best practice advice on how to effectively lead global teams.

Doyle congratulated Jones on his new position and gave his inquiry careful consideration. After several minutes of non-specific conversation, Doyle responded that she honestly could not pinpoint her company's best practices for leading global project and program teams. She certainly agreed that her company was a leader in globalization strategy and execution, but she could not identify the handful of things that constitute their leadership position. She went on to explain that working in highly distributed teams was just how they did things at her company, and it is how they have been creating their products for over 20 years. They began working in highly distributed development teams long before most other companies came to realize that doing so could provide a competitive advantage. Distributed teams are merely a component of their company culture, Doyle concluded.

This conversation led Jones to realize that Keytron was a globalization follower, not a globalization leader, and that he and his company were playing a game of catch-up to the globalization leaders within the consumer electronics industry. In fact, they were just beginning the transition process from a domestic-focused company to a global-focused company, and as such they were experiencing problems associated with leading highly distributed teams. Even though they were now operating in a global environment, the company's business processes, tools, and organizational and team structures were still based on a local development model in which much of the work was performed at a single site and within a common business and country culture. Additionally, the global project team leaders working for

Jones were struggling to overcome the cultural, communication, time zone, and distributed virtual team challenges they were now facing.

As a result, Keytron's development teams seemed to be in disarray. Poor cross-team communication was causing severe development delays, poor documentation and disjointed work hand-offs were resulting in mistakes and rework, and a breakdown in trust had occurred due to continual finger-pointing, scapegoating, and blame for missed deliverables and goals. Additionally, organizational, functional, and geographic silos were causing a focus on local solutions instead of a single globally-integrated product solution. To make matters worse, a recent investment in a suite of new software-based collaborative tools has failed to improve the situation, and may actually be making it worse by diverting attention away from some of the core problems causing the poor global execution. Needless to say, Keytron's product development performance is at risk and therefore their strategic goal to be one of the world's top consumer electronics companies is in jeopardy despite their growth strategy of targeted mergers and acquisitions of other companies.

Jones's predicament is not an isolated case. Like many others today, he finds himself in a business environment that is becoming increasingly more complex as organizations attempt to grow their firms globally. As a result, conventional ways of developing products and services that he has become familiar with during his career are no longer effective – Jones is feeling the pressures of globalization.

Are you feeling the pressures of globalization? If your answer is "no," you may not be paying close enough attention to your market, industry, customers, workforce, and the trends associated with each. It has been argued that our globe is quickly becoming smaller, flatter, and thus creating a more level playing field for organizational work.[1] The pressures caused by competition for global market share and for the world's most talented people, and the sheer desire for competitive advantage, fuel these occurrences. In this century, organizational leaders in every sector of every business must look globally for knowledge, skills, and abilities to achieve improved business results. The intellectual skills necessary for creative thinking and innovation as well as production and operational abilities are available and ready for use for any organization from around the world. Many of them have already been tapped by companies that are successfully executing their globalization strategies, some of these companies might be your direct competitors. So, we ask again, are you feeling the pressures of globalization?

For some of you reading this, these words ring all too true and you are in search of answers for effective globalization practices. Keep reading, many of your concerns will be addressed. For those not realizing the pressures and effects of globalization, keep reading as well because you will gain an awareness of globalization and an increased understanding of the power of this evolutionary shift.

Globalization Forces

The idea of globalization is not a recent revolutionary occurrence, but rather an evolution started centuries ago that is still evolving today. Visionary leaders have recognized that competitive advantages can be gained over their rivals with an effective globalization strategy. This is especially true when coupled with an equally effective global execution model. Current globalization leaders have established a recognizable competitive advantage in their respective industries, but it should also be recognized that their competitive advantage was not established overnight. In fact, globalization leaders have spent many years and have learned many hard lessons establishing their global business models. In contrast, newcomers to the globalization game – which we call globalization followers – are in many cases being forced into the global arena in order to compete with and survive against the globalization leaders. It is within the organizations of the globalization followers that we see the greatest challenges and barriers to effective global team leadership.

To be an effective senior manager or global team leader in today's global marketplace requires one to become competent in global business acumen and to develop a world view. Global business acumen includes the ability to comprehend our business environment in its entirety. A world view refers to developing an awareness of the global environment to include social, political, and economic trends[2]. The prospective global team leader must be able to apply their previously acquired knowledge, skills and competencies within this global context.

Globalization does not have a singular cause or influence, but rather is driven by a set of forces that have operated interdependently throughout recent history. Knowledge of the three primary globalization forces – economic forces, political forces, and technology forces – provides senior managers and global team leaders a greater context of the environment in which they operate. This greater context can help free the global team leader from feeling as though the global challenges they face are a result of poor senior management decision making, but rather part of the dynamic environment within which all global businesses operate.

Economic Forces

The basis of global economics involves the creation of economic interrelations across geographical boundaries as defined by national borders through the production, exchange, and consumption of goods and services[3]. Global free-market economics is stimulated by the flow of money and capital between nations by large and small transnational corporations, international economic institutions, and trading systems that create interdependencies between national economies.

World economics of the past several centuries has been dominated by two philosophies: free-market economics and Keynesian economics. Free-market economics is rooted in the view of Adam Smith (1723-1790) who defined markets as self-regulating mechanisms that drive toward a balance between supply and demand of goods and services.[4] Within a free-market system, trade in goods and services between nations is unhindered by government-imposed restrictions such as taxes, tariffs, and quotas. Free-market economics is characterized by free access to markets, free movement of labor between nations, and free movement of capital between nations.

Keynesian economics, conversely, advocates nation-state influence of world economic policy. John Maynard Keynes (1883-1946) believed that economic systems would not automatically balance by themselves; therefore, macro-economic control by government institutions is needed to ensure balance and equity within an economy. This includes control of money supply, control of interest rates, and control of market access. Keynesian theory recognizes that economic systems will realize points of downturn and even depression and that these systems are not self-correcting, but rather need support from government to boost the system in recovery.[5]

Today, the three most notable, and arguably most influential, global economic institutions that were born out of Keynesian economics are the International Monetary Fund, the World Bank, and the World Trade Organization. The International Monetary Fund and World Bank were created near the end of World War II to administer an international monetary system and to fund development projects in developing countries. The International Monetary Fund oversees the global financial system by observing exchange rates as well as offering financial and technical assistance. The World Bank is an internationally supported bank that provides loans to developing countries for development programs.[6] The World Trade Organization was created in 1995 as the successor to the General Agreement on Tariffs and Trade to deal with the rules of trade between nations and is responsible for negotiating and implementing new trade agreements between countries.[7] These three institutions continue to be instrumental in influencing the rules of the global economy by controlling international monetary and trade policy.

Whether dominated by free-market policy, Keynesian policy, or a combination of the two – which is dominant today – economics is the primary force behind globalization. It is economics that drives the world's entrepreneurs and globalization leaders to seek new markets for their goods and services, to find new suppliers for their raw materials, to develop world-wide sources for production and distribution, and generally to evaluate the world's resources for potential competitive advantage and product optimization.

Political Forces

World politics is the second primary force that drives globalization. Economic globalization forces have rarely been able to operate independently from political forces. Most often global economic expansion and contraction is set in motion by a series of political actions. The basis of world politics is the generation, distribution, and control of power and influence.[8] For many centuries, control of power has been achieved by creating territorial lines that defined national borders. In doing so, artificial boundaries have been created that allow us to view the world as a series of 'domestic' and 'foreign' relationships.

The political force pressuring globalization involves the partial permeation of these national boundaries in order to expand the trade of goods and services. Fledgling entrepreneurs have not been able to achieve expansion of their businesses on a global basis without the support of their governments and of the governments of their trading partners; for example, the three major economic institutions described above were all spawned as a result of the formation of new global political policy following World War II to support localized business for global purposes. Without a supportive political environment and policies, these institutions would not have been formed nor would they have been successful in carrying out their missions.

The direction of globalization is generally guided by the political agendas of the world's most influential nations. Governments play an extensive role in globalization by exerting their political agendas through the opening and closing of markets that entrepreneurs and globalization leaders can leverage through the investment in technology research and development.

While recently we have seen the world influenced by the decisions of the Global-20, over the past 50 years, governments (primary the United States and Russian governments) have funded the early development of technologies that were later commercialized and are now common in our personal and work lives today. Many of these advancements came out of the competition and conflict between the United States and Russian governments in trying to win the race to the moon and to win the Cold War. Today, we are witnessing competitive business wars beyond Russia and the United States. Businesses from around the world are competing to be first to market with a sustainable product base and growing customer demand. Those with the most compelling offerings and most effective globalization strategy/execution combination will win, and the followers will be forced to resort to reactive strategies for survival.

Technology Forces

Technology is the third primary globalization force. While economics is the true driving force for globalization and politics is mainly a guiding force that either stimulates or contracts globalization, technology is the force that makes globalization both more effective and efficient. Said another way, the *speed* of globalization is dependent upon the conditions for technological use and advancement of technology development.

21

The basis of technology as a globalization force is in the development and dissemination of new ways to expand our global reach, to facilitate the interaction and interdependencies of humans across the globe, and to enable the flow of monetary exchange across national borders.

Early technology development focused on more effective forms of transportation to help explorers overcome geographical barriers which prevented them from opening new trade routes to expand their markets. Later, new power technologies helped to make transportation of goods and services much more efficient by tapping new power sources such as coal, steam, and petroleum.[9] This led to the invention of mechanized shipping, railway systems, and automotive and air transportation. Additionally, the introduction of electricity spawned new communication technologies such as the telegraph, telephone, electronic money exchange, radio, and television.

Today, much technological development has been focused on the introduction of collaborative technologies that have resulted in further permeation of national boundaries to the point where national boundaries no longer prevent people from collaborating and participating in the exchange of goods and services. These include internet technologies, business-to-business e-commerce technologies, and workflow technologies that enable knowledge work to be disaggregated, distributed, and re-integrated across the globe. Collectively recognized as technology, this force speeds the rate at which globalization can expand through the use of various technological advancements.

Interaction of Globalization Forces

Although it helps to look at each of the three primary forces of globalization separately to better understand their influence on globalization, the forces themselves do not operate independently. It is the interaction of economic, political, and technological forces that has historically had the most dramatic influence on globalization.

We use the tri-circle model shown in Figure 1-1 to graphically demonstrate the interactions between the globalization forces and the resulting impacts on the world economies. We provide this analysis to help the global team leader become more aware of the dynamic forces in play within the environment that their project or program operates.

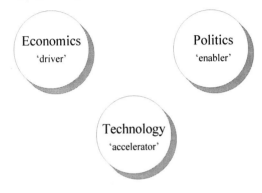

Figure 1-1: The primary globalization forces

Globalization can be characterized by drivers, enablers, and accelerators. Economics is the globalization *driver*, meaning the quest for greater economic gain has fueled the human desire to connect with others across the globe to expand the production and sales of goods and services primarily for prosperity, but also for human connection.

Politics is the globalization *enabler*. Political policy is driven by the agendas of the world's nation-state leaders, which in turn either positively or negatively affects global economic interconnection between nations.

The third force, technology, is the globalization *accelerator*. Historically, significant advances in various technologies have increased the pace in which people and economies have become interconnected.

When the globalization forces are independent in nature, as demonstrated in Figure 1-1, it represents a period of slow globalization expansion or, more likely, globalization contraction. When the globalization forces become highly integrated, as demonstrated in Figure 1-2, a state of globalization exists where all three forces are at work to facilitate the wide and rapid expansion of globalization. Such is the state of globalization today, where world economics and monetary exchange are driving globalization, political stability and alignment are enabling continued globalization into new and larger markets, and the advent of new work-flow technologies has accelerated knowledge work activities, allowing work to be disaggregated at it's source, distributed digitally to workers across the globe, worked on by geographically dispersed specialists, and then reintegrated into a new solution back at the source or at some other location in the world.[10]

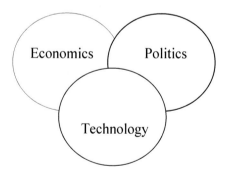

Figure 1-2: Integration of the globalization forces

The modern expansion of globalization has been further accelerated by satellite and fiber optic communication technologies that have served to connect computer systems, businesses, and people around the world. Trillions of dollars are now exchanged across the globe each year via the internet alone. As well, computerization and collaboration technologies have digitized the world causing massive change in the way we communicate and work. In 1990, email was virtually unknown. Less than two decades later, electronic communication technology allows for the immediate distribution of information virtually everywhere, instantly.

Because of these technologies, the pace of globalization has once again accelerated. The form of globalization today, however, is different. The new collaborative technologies have enabled the digitization of knowledge work across the entire product or service development lifecycle – from ideation to final delivery to the customer.

The integration of the globalization forces is causing changes that will continue for the foreseeable future even though there will be continual resistance to the trend as well as constant challenges associated with executing in a global environment. For those of us caught in the changing tide, it is time to adjust our perspective and sharpen our skills to ensure our personal success – and the success of our companies – in this current wave of massive globalization.

Why Globalize?

The short answer to the question "why globalize?" is survival and sustainability. Most senior leaders have realized the need to become a part of the global marketplace, and in many cases have developed strategies to move their organizations into the global arena. These strategies include developing strategic alliances with overseas development and marketing partners, off-shoring and outsourcing of their product or service development processes to outside firms that can perform the work more efficiently, moving portions of their operations into foreign countries to enter new markets and acquire new talent, and acquiring other companies in other parts of the world that complement and expand their business. These strategies of course have created a trend away from co-located development teams and toward highly distributed teams.

But what is the real driver for this distribution of work? The most common belief is that it is to reduce the development and manufacturing costs of products and services; however, when one digs deeper into this claim, you discover that reduction of cost is but one of three primary business strategies that are used by leading companies to gain competitive advantage through globalization of their business – all of which result in highly distributed workforces.

The three primary globalization business strategies are the following:

1. Reduction of product and service cost driven by lowering development and manufacturing cost;

2. Expansion of product and service sales into local, emerging markets; and

3. Employment and retention of the world's top talent to create and develop new products and services.

Globalization Strategy One: Reducing Cost

Historically, the most common reason cited for globalization is to reduce development and manufacturing costs. Companies have been off-shoring their manufacturing work for several decades to take advantage of low cost labor and advanced automation. For many companies, this is now a normal part of their business practices. The new frontier in cost reduction is in the off-shoring and outsourcing of a company's design work as a strategic method to reduce research and development cost.

Leading companies have become quite proficient at developing their product and services in a highly distributed model that spans the globe, and have established competitive cost advantages over their rivals for more than a decade by integrating the global model into their core business practices. As a result, these companies use a cost reduction strategy less frequently today.[11] As the saying goes, they have "been there and done that." However, this is only true for the globalization leaders, and is not the case for companies that are globalization followers.

Globalization followers are being forced to employ a cost-reduction globalization strategy in order to remain competitive with the globalization leaders by taking advantage of lower-cost labor or advanced manufacturing automation in other geographies from which they are based. In this case, the primary strategy is reactive and defensive in nature as they are being pulled into globalization as a means of lowering product and service development cost to protect against being forced out of markets based on price. Such is the case, for example, of InFocus Corporation. Once the world leader in business projection technologies, InFocus was forced to lower its product cost in order to stay competitive with the globalization leaders in office products such as NEC and Panasonic. They have mostly failed in their attempts to lower their product cost through a reactive globalization strategy to move their manufacturing and various parts of product design to countries with a lower cost of labor. As a result, they have moved from being a domestic leader in their industry to a global follower, and are currently on the cusp of being driven out of the industry all together.

The danger with a reactive globalization strategy is that when we react we do not necessarily calculate risk versus benefit adequately, or thoroughly map out a plan of action. As a result, the reactive strategy many times ends up being more costly and time consuming for the organization.

Globalization Strategy Two: Expansion into Emerging Markets

The wants and needs of customers within developing nations and emerging markets are many times much different than those of a company's mainstream markets. It becomes difficult to define and design products and services that will meet the needs of developing and emerging market customers without in-depth intelligence of that particular customer base. To gain this required intelligence, companies are employing the strategy of hiring individuals within the emerging markets they plan to serve to define and design their new products and services. As one participant in a BusinessWeek study on global product and service development stated:[12]

> *"No one understands the local customers as well as the people we have within those markets."*

In other cases, government policy requires companies to establish an investment in a local market before it is allowed to sell its products and services into that market. This investment often takes the form of establishing a local operation and hiring people within the market to participate in the design, development, and manufacturing of a company's products and services.

This global expansion strategy is primarily used by the globalization leaders as they capture the lion's share of their primary markets and seek to open up new markets for their products and services. The result of this global strategy is a distributed network of people who will be formed into development teams chartered to produce products and services to be sold into that emerging market. The obstacles here include learning new languages, cultures, and developing new policies – none of which are easy to overcome by most companies.

Globalization Strategy Three: Acquiring the World's Top Talent

For many companies, acquiring the world's top talent and relocating them to the company's home base has become much more challenging today than just a few short years ago. Two significant factors are at the source of this challenge: world terrorism and growing employment opportunities in developing nations.

Largely due to the threat of terrorism, the United States and other western governments have severely restricted the number of work permits and citizenship opportunities to foreigners. Further, there are new restrictions on the length of stay in the country for foreign nationals looking to immigrate to these countries. Collectively, this restricts the number of foreign workers that companies can bring to the country each year and prevents access to some of the world's best and brightest people.

The increase in prosperity and associated growth in availability of work for highly skilled and educated workers in countries such as India, Taiwan, China, Brazil, and Russia has made it possible for workers from these countries to remain home and establish a standard of living as high, or higher, than they could enjoy by moving abroad. This means that the supply of highly skilled workers willing to immigrate to countries in North America and Europe is continuing to decline.

Companies that have been leading the modern globalization movement have seen this trend for several years, and have enacted strategies to move portions of their operations to the highly skilled workers abroad. Large satellite operations of North American and European companies can now be found in cities around the world that have a large concentration of highly skilled workers. These cities include Bangalore, Shanghai, Sao Paulo, and Moscow to name but a few.

Other companies that have been slow to establish globalization strategies have begun to feel the pinch for highly skilled workers. Once again, these companies find themselves having to establish a reactionary strategy to set up operations within foreign countries that they have had limited or no experience with to date in order to attract the skilled workers they need to compete in the global marketplace.

Globalization Strategy and Global Execution

As previously mentioned, senior leaders in organizations have realized the need to become part of the global marketplace, and have executed various strategies to move their companies into the global arena. For some, the strategies have been well executed. For most, however, senior leaders and their staff are realizing that good strategy is not good enough. Changes in globalization strategy have to be accompanied by changes in global execution. Within an organization, focus must quickly shift from the development and initiation of their globalization strategies to operational success in developing their products and services in a global model.

This is where many senior leaders and their organizations fail. They fail to redesign and realign their execution processes, tools, structures, practices, and skills for operation in a highly distributed and global environment. This failure has caused the global execution problems that are common today.

Caught in the middle of the misalignment between globalization strategy and poor global execution are the middle managers and project or program team leaders who are trying to sew globalization strategy and global execution together from the middle of the organization. Unfortunately, this is a daunting and nearly impossible task.

Like Scott Jones, who was introduced at the beginning of this chapter, team leaders often find that they now have to lead product and service development teams that are distributed across the globe. Unfortunately, many of these leaders are not equipped or prepared to deal with some of the significant barriers and challenges they encounter while leading their global project and program teams.

Looking Ahead

In this opening chapter, we looked at the primary forces that drive either the expansion or contraction of globalization, and demonstrated how the current integration of these forces – economics, politics, and technology – is providing an environment for driving companies further into globalization as a means to remain competitive within their industries.

Many companies that have adopted a globalization strategy, however, have found that the road to the fulfillment of anticipated business results is paved with unanticipated execution problems and barriers. In the next chapter, we uncover and discuss in detail the primary barriers and challenges to success that are commonly encountered by both senior managers and global project and program team leaders as they try to lead globally-distributed product and service development teams within an organizational environment that was initially optimized for non-distributed work.

CHAPTER TWO

Barriers and Challenges to Global Success

"The greatest difficulty in the world is not for people to accept new ideas, but to make them forget their old ideas."
- John Maynard Keynes

As theorists and practitioners continue to descriptively label the global business arena as small, flat, and level, there is an increased understanding that these adjectives are not synonymous with fast, easy, or effective relative to global business execution. Unfortunately, these lessons are being learned through failed attempts to operationalize global workforce practices costing organizations significant amounts of money, market share, and opportunity.

Such failed attempts, however, have not deterred senior managers within product and service development companies from continuing to pursue a globalization strategy. This is evidenced by the fact that eighty-three percent of the senior leaders who have expressed serious failures in their global execution efforts foresee an increase, not a decrease, in their globalization programs over the next five years.[1] These senior leaders clearly still believe the globalization benefits exceed the barriers and challenges to success that they are encountering during the transition process from a domestic to a global business.

Most senior leaders who embark on a globalization strategy fail to anticipate, estimate, or adequately address the number and severity of barriers and problems that will be encountered during project or program execution in a globally distributed environment. We refer to this as the misalignment between globalization strategy and global execution.

We purposefully distinguish between global execution barriers and challenges for two primary reasons: First, it is important to delineate responsibilities between senior managers and global project or program team leaders. Senior managers of an organization are best positioned to address the global execution barriers. The global team leaders are best positioned to address the global execution challenges. Secondly, we distinguish between the two to underscore the point that global execution barriers should be addressed first, and with priority effort, before expectations are set for a firm's team leaders to make progress on resolving the global team challenges. Without removal of the barriers, global team leaders will be hard pressed to resolve the global execution challenges.

In this chapter, we describe the most common global execution barriers and challenges that are encountered by global product and service development companies and their execution teams. Overcoming these barriers and challenges is necessary to establishing alignment between business strategy and execution output in a global setting. This alignment is what separates the leading global companies from the global followers.

Global Execution Barriers

We define global execution barriers as fundamental organizational structures, power bases, and behaviors that prevent companies from effectively operating in a global environment. A series of organizational, operational, and philosophical changes must occur in order to prepare and enable an organization to move from a domestic or locally-focused product and service development model to a globally-focused model. Without these fundamental shifts, effective global execution is severely challenged as are the business results intended. The most common and significant global execution barriers are the following:

1. Organizational structures and performance measures that limit the collaborative team dynamics that are necessary in a global development model;

2. Differences in culture – country, company, and functional – that are not appropriately characterized, understood, and assimilated into the organization;

3. A development model that does not support the highly collaborative and interdependent nature of global product and service development activities;

4. Skills and competencies of project and program team leaders that have not kept pace with the more comprehensive set of skills and competencies needed to be successful in the global environment; and

5. Senior management support for global transition change management programs.

Structures and Performance Measures

Simply stated, successful global team execution depends upon effective collaboration between team members. Creating sustainable and repeatable success in global product and service development lies in a firm's ability to assemble, deploy, and lead a flexible network of resources who work in a variety of collaborative arrangements to accomplish the desired mission and business goals.[2] The ability to transform an organization to work in this new model in which resources are distributed, highly interdependent, and focused on a common goal is both a key to success of the global leaders and a primary barrier to success for the global followers.

In order to succeed, global organizations need to have the right structures, people, processes, and technologies that foster a high degree of collaboration. Many senior leaders who have embarked on a globalization strategy that embraces multiple nations and geographies have run into this execution barrier because they have failed to deemphasize the barriers between the functional silos within their own organizations. These barriers can manifest themselves as either functional discipline barriers or sub-optimized objectives which span the business segments of the enterprise. Global leaders have obtained success in the global environment by shifting to a flatter, less hierarchical organizational structure that enables team members to make decisions on local information, but in alignment with a common team vision and set of enterprise-wide goals.[3]

Most large, complex organizations with traditional, power-driven structures are cauldrons of competing interests and competing commitments that encourage and reward individualism and foster unhealthy competition among members and between functions.

As one can see from Figure 2-1, traditional organization hierarchies are vertically structured with well-defined boundaries between the functions. The boundaries between groups within these organizations exist naturally because silos, by definition, pursue different goals and tasks. As the result of the well-defined boundaries and inward-looking goals, each function has a narrow span of control. Additionally, leaders of these

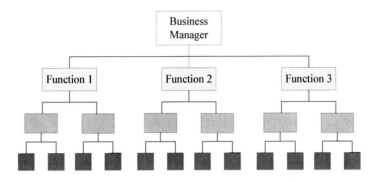

Figure 2-1: A typical hierarchical organization structure

organizations tend to be distant, separate entities that are hard to reach and disconnected from the operational workings of the organization.[4] In such a structure, it is very difficult for a global team leader to effectively drive a high degree of cross-organizational collaboration. The structure itself and the management behavior that it enables become the limiting factors to collaboration success.

This is a situation in which Kevin Johnson learned with great pain to his self-esteem and professional ego. Johnson was hired by the CEO of a consulting services company as the new Director of Program Management with a task of getting the functional departments within the company to work more collaboratively as they begin to expand globally. The CEO chose Johnson as his new director because of his previous experience working in a similar manner for a company consistently recognized as a global leader within its industry.

Originally, Johnson was excited with the prospect of being able to take a traditionally silo-oriented organization and transform it into a collaborative and high performing team. Over the course of the next year, however, Johnson's excitement turned into increased frustration and eventual disdain for his new employer.

The power base within each of the functions, or silos, was so well established that Johnson was unable to prevent the continual turf wars in order to appropriately influence the organization to work toward common and collective goals. Each time Johnson brought the issue to the attention of the CEO, he was told that the department managers were 'strong-willed old boys' and that the CEO would have a talk with them.

Eventually the CEO's talks may have had an effect on the department managers because in at least one instance they *did* collaborate. As a group, they convinced the CEO that Johnson was well intended, but just did not fit into the culture of the company and would be forever viewed as an outsider. Completely discredited by this move, Johnson was subsequently asked to resign from the company. He did resign, and to this day the company remains a global follower steeped in cross-silo power struggles.

In order to prevent situations similar to the one above, a couple things need to happen. First, the senior leader of an organization must drive all changes necessary to de-emphasize strong organizational silos that consistently create barriers to global execution success. The senior leader cannot realistically push this responsibility lower within the organization. Second, a change in performance measures and rewards must follow a change in organization structure in order to change the behaviors of people operating in a global product and service development model. Hierarchical, silo-focused organizations tend to reward individual accomplishments over team accomplishments (unless of course the team resides within a single organizational silo). They in fact shift focus from achievement of a common vision to achievement of individual goals. In a global execution model where success is dependent upon cross-functional, cross-cultural collaboration, individual performance measures and rewards need to be based primarily on achievement of team goals and secondarily on individual results.

When people on a global project or program team are working collaboratively toward a common set of goals, they cannot be rewarded for competing against one another. Instead, they need to be measured and rewarded based upon team progress and accomplishment.[5] In a like manner, functional managers cannot be rewarded for achieving the goals that are specific to their function alone. Organizational goals are always important, but functional manager support for and contribution to the success of the firm's global project or program teams must be the first priority for rewards and recognition.

Differences in Country, Company, and Functional Culture

As a company embarks on a globalization strategy, it employs various tactics to expand beyond its current national boundaries. Some of the most common tactics include acquiring or merging with companies in other parts of the world, forming strategic partnerships with other companies to share and distribute portions of the development delivery system, and expanding operational components of its business into other geographical regions of the world.

Regardless of the strategy and associated tactics, one of the results is common – the organization expands its pool of resources to include people from other cultures, thus becoming a multi-cultural entity. When doing so, it therefore must undergo various forms of transformation to effectively and efficiently create a new organizational environment that embraces, encompasses, and leverages its new cultural diversity. This will require changes in the organizational values, norms, assumptions, and how individuals and teams interact with one another.

Failure to fully transform a company from a single or limited cultural entity to a blended culture consistently creates the second significant barrier to global execution success: misalignment of national, company, and functional culture. Most companies either underestimate or completely ignore the amount of time and attention needed to blend the cultural components of its workforce when it embarks on a globalization strategy.

This failure by senior managers within a firm consistently creates a complex and many times contentious environment in which the global project and program team leaders must execute. An environment, in which cultural values, assumptions, and ways of working and doing business, vary will cause conflict with the traditional ways of operating in a project or program team environment if not identified, addressed, and resolved. Worse yet, the diverse values, norms, and assumptions may conflict with the project or program team's goals that leaves attainment of the goals in jeopardy.

One manager described his recent experience with this problem during our research. After earning his business degree from Clemson University, James Turk accepted a position with a worldwide apparel company. The organization has over 400 facilities including eleven manufacturing locations and eight distribution centers around the world. Working out of the Cincinnati office, Turk proved to be a quick study of the industry and was noticed as a rising star in the company. Within five years, he was promoted to a director position – the youngest named director in the company's history.

Shortly after his promotion, Turk was asked to take on a special project. The project was to open and operate a new sourcing and manufacturing center in Hong Kong. Today, Turk has been in Hong Kong for nearly five years and has built the sourcing and manufacturing center to operate efficiently and effectively. He recently took time to discuss his transition as an American educated in an American university and now running a successful international business operation in China.

As he contemplated the criteria of global management success, he suggested that "the most important factor is culture." Universities and corporate educational settings can do a fine job explaining expectations and theoretical scenarios through role playing or simulations. However, this is akin to explaining to someone how to swim if they never have swum before. The best way to learn is to experience the real thing.

"The real thing," as Turk explained, "is either slightly or very different than the way it was taught in a training course. This is not to say the training is bad, wrong, or unnecessary. Quite the opposite is true. The trainings allow you to start the awareness process. This process is not complete, however, when you leave the training with a certificate of completion in hand. The process is exactly that, *a process,* and therefore is ongoing. Anyone engaged in worldwide endeavors – especially international management – understands the intricacies of cultures and associated rituals and ceremonies, all of which are important to understand especially when you are an American running a business in China – the opposite is true as well."

Turk went on to explain that cross-cultural managers must be knowledgeable about cultural economic situations, individual motives and preferences, language, values, appropriate expressions, and be politically savvy and legally adept at analyzing the geographic and business situation. But according to Turk as well as many other international managers with whom we talked, one of the most important concerns is cultural awareness. "Understanding culture is a critically important aspect of global business and, from an American perspective, the biggest mistake made by U.S. companies is not providing the necessary cultural awareness training to ensure that their personnel are as culturally savvy as possible," explained Turk. "Most U.S. managers push their business model onto others and force their culture and way of business overseas. I have not seen this approach work successfully. This is especially true in Asia."

So then, why does cultural diversification create a potential barrier to success for global project and program teams? The answer is *complexity.* A domestic project or program team leader normally needs only to concern himself or herself with one set of cultural paradigms. A global team leader by contrast must expand his or her knowledge and competency to include multiple cultural values, norms, and assumptions that all come in to play simultaneously.[6] Team leaders must constantly guard against falling prey to cultural misperception and projected similarity, assuming that all people and their corresponding situations are identical or similar to theirs.[7]

To complicate things further, culture is multi-dimensional. When we think of cultural diversity, most of us first think of national culture: differences in people due to nationality or country of origin. The global team leader cannot lead his or her project team with an ethnocentric mindset that is focused on his or her nation of origin – to do so will likely cause serious damage to the team and the organization as a whole. Minimally, the global team leader must be aware of national cultural aspects concerning gender, religion, national holidays, conflict management, individualism versus collectivism, and tolerance for ambiguity.

This is a lesson that Scott Jones from Keytron Electronics learned within the first few months of his new position as Director of Product Development. It was brought to his attention by one of his product development program managers that a member of her program team did an outstanding job of stewarding the first version of the product through the manufacturing process. Jones decided the team member was deserving of special recognition and reward, and chose to publicly recognize the team member on the company website and in a department meeting. "I did not yet understand that this very typical recognition that I had used many times for domestic, United States-based teams, was quite inappropriate for globally-distributed teams," explained Jones. "Since this person was from a collective culture, to be singled out for credit in front of his entire team, each of whom also had contributed to the team's success, was not a rewarding experience at all. In fact, this gesture was a humiliating and de-motivating experience for this individual who lived and worked in China."

It is quite common today to find that many members of global project and program teams were once part of another company altogether, and came to their existing company by way of a corporate merger or acquisition. Since each company has its own corporate culture consisting of unique values and ways of doing business, company culture must also be managed within the blended global team environment. The leaders of the global organization must establish the norms and guidelines within which the global teams must operate such as who should make various decisions, what decision-making method is preferred, how much risk the organization is willing to tolerate, what development methods, processes, and tools will be utilized, and how the company will operate within its competitive environment.

Developing products and services involves combining team members with diverse functional expertise such as sales and marketing, engineering, quality assurance, customer support, and so on. Experts within each of these functions develop their own practices, ways of doing business, and biases that may affect the global project or program team.[8] This is known as functional culture, and is the third dimension of culture that global organizations and teams have to contend with. Multiple viewpoints from each of the functions involved in global product and service development must be comprehended and blended in order to achieve cross-functional collaboration. This means that the opinions and functional-specific methods must be valued and leveraged equally within the organization and on the project or program teams.

Managing across cultures therefore entails much more than managing the obvious differences in backgrounds and language. It involves the ability to blend national, company, and functional culture in a way which promotes collaboration and collective thinking. The blended culture must then be aligned with a common vision and set of global projects or program goals in order to effectively execute a global strategy.

Collaborative Development Model

Many times, a firm's product or service development model is heavily influenced by the type of organizational structure established within the firm. A hierarchical, functionally silo-oriented organization often employs a project hand-off development model where work is accomplished by one functional team, then passed to the next functional team to complete its work, and so on. One such company is Hospi-Tek, a medical devices manufacturing company who has historically used a project hand-off development model (Figure 2-1) to create its products.[9]

Under the historical project hand-off method, the Hospi-Tek product development effort began with the architectural team who developed the architectural concept and derived the high-level requirements of the medical device from the work of the product marketing team. The architectural concept and specification were then handed off to the hardware engineering team who assumed ownership of the project. The engineering team developed the hardware and software requirements, engineering specifications, and the product design, which were then handed off to the manufacturing team who assumed ownership of the project. The manufacturing team developed the manufacturing processes, retooled the factory, and produced the physical product. The product and project ownership were then handed off to the validation and test team who performed product and component level testing to ensure the product achieved the functional, quality, usability, and reliability requirements.

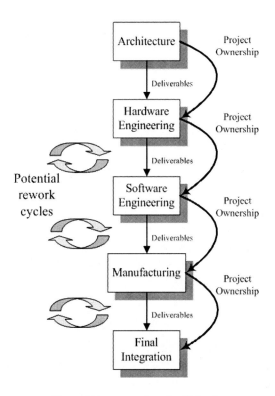

Figure 2-2: Hospi-Tek project hand-off development model

Unfortunately, this development model is not scaleable, and as a company begins to succeed and grow, product and process complexity begin to render the development model ineffective and inefficient. The primary problem occurs when errors are introduced and missed at an early stage of development and have to be reconciled and fixed downstream, resulting in multiple rework cycles that consume time-to-money advantage.

This was the case when Hospi-Tek tried to apply this historic project hand-off development model as it began to globalize its business. The complexity created by a highly distributed team with representatives in multiple geographies caused a complete break-down of the project hand-off development model. The first two globally developed products failed to meet their launch and quality targets, failed to meet market timing, and therefore failed to achieve the business results intended.

Global product and service development requires a development model that facilitates a high degree of horizontal collaboration, synchronization, iteration, communication, and integration throughout the entire development lifecycle (see Chapter Three). This is because success in a highly-distributed model is achieved by identifying, understanding and managing the interdependencies between the team that spans organizational functions, geographical boundaries, cultures, and time zones. With a flatter organizational structure, the opportunity exists to institute a new product or service development model that takes advantage of cross-organization collaboration.

Global Team Leader Skills and Competencies

As firms begin developing products and services in a globally distributed environment, the senior leaders of a firm must ensure that their team leaders are adequately skilled and competent to overcome the significant complexities that a globally-distributed virtual team presents. The primary complexities that must be overcome include the following: [10]

- Crossing boundaries related to time, distance, and organization;

- Communicating and collaborating using technology;

- Working in a multi-cultural environment; and

- Preventing misunderstandings and conflict between team members who do not share a common first language.

There are many documented instances where a project manager with a good track record of leading co-located or domestic teams fails horribly when moved to leading a globally-distributed team. It should be understood that this is not usually the fault of the project manager; rather, it is the fault of the senior managers of the organization for not recognizing that they need a team leader that possesses a broader skill set and experience to effectively lead a virtual team as compared to those needed for leading a co-located team.

Leading effectively in the complex virtual team environment requires project and program team leaders who possess specialized competencies. These competencies include basic project management techniques, program management knowledge and experience, networking across functional, hierarchical, and organizational boundaries, use of electronic communication and collaboration technologies, and effective management across time zones. The team leader must also utilize her or her interpersonal awareness skills to work toward blending cultural differences. Of utmost importance is the ability to integrate a team across the globe by creating a common vision of success and aligning the integrated team and its work processes to the vision.

Additionally, global team leaders need to have a broad understanding of the global business environment and of the cultures within which they operate. They must possess personal qualities that help them lead a diverse and widely-distributed team and set of stakeholders. Finally, leading global project and program teams cannot be learned in a classroom or from reading a book, it has to be practiced. Improvement comes with a history of successes and failures associated with actually leading global teams and true evidence of competence comes from a track record of proven accomplishments that represents an individual's experience base.

Indeed, it is the responsibility of the senior manager of an organization to ensure that they have adequately skilled and experienced individuals to lead their global teams. This includes hiring seasoned global team leaders if none exist within the organization when it first begins to develop products and services globally. It also includes identifying good candidates that can be grown into a global team leader role through training and mentoring, and ensuring an on-going training and career development program is in place to continually increase competency.

An associated barrier to success can exist if the global project or program team leader is not adequately empowered to operate and lead the global team in the role that he or she is expected to fulfill. Senior leaders within the organization must formally empower the global team leaders with the appropriate levels of delegation for decision-making power and authority that are commensurate with their level of responsibility which enables them to lead across the functional silos of an enterprise.

Senior Management Support for Global Transition

Embarking on a globalization strategy sets an organization on a path of significant change. Unfortunately, many managers spend a considerable amount of time and effort contemplating their globalization strategy, but spend much less time thinking about the scope of organizational change that will be required to realize the goals of that strategy. In addition, it is all too common for the senior leadership to delegate the global transition change tactics to lower levels of the organization and then take a personal hands-off approach.

Greater success is realized when senior managers stay personally involved in and fully supportive of the structural and operational elements of a global transition. This involves communicating the need and details of the various transitions that will occur, providing the resources necessary, staying actively engaged in the decision process, and working to remove barriers to the success of those actively implementing the changes within the organization.

Susan DePinto is feeling the effects of poor senior management support for her global transition project. Recent actions by the senior executive of the business unit for which she works has greatly increased the risk that the transition program she leads will fail to meet its goals.

DePinto works for a support organization within a well known global financial institution. The current economic climate – characterized as a global recession – has forced the organization to develop a global strategy based on cost reduction to ensure the institution remains financially viable. One of the cost reduction actions is to move many of the support services which currently exist in North America and Europe to service centers that exist in two lower-cost countries. The company currently has small operations in each of the off-shore sites, both of which have proven to be successful due to a fairly mature communication infrastructure and an adequately-skilled workforce. The strategy, therefore, is to move additional and more complex services into these two offshore locations and shut down redundant services in North America and Europe.

DePinto explained her role in the global transition: "Each of the off-shore service centers has been running as a separate entity with unique structures, processes, policies, and workforce roles and responsibilities. I'm responsible for consolidating the two service centers as a single, global entity with a common structure, processes, policies, and roles and responsibilities. I will then lead the analysis of services to determine which will transition to the new global service center and which will remain in North America and Europe, and finally I'll oversee the transition change management program to ensure the transition is transparent to the overall workforce of the company."

News of the transition was released by the senior executive of the organization, which sparked a lot of questions and emotions by members of the workforce. Even though the senior executive announced the global services transition strategy, details of the business reasons behind the transition, the decisions supporting the strategy, and information on which employees will be impacted and when they will be impacted have never been formally communicated to the workforce – especially to the employees located in North America and Europe. "This, of course, has created a significant amount of angst for the organization's workforce," explained DePinto.

In a recent business update meeting for the European employees, the senior executive for the business unit became frustrated with the emotional questions coming from the employees who were concerned with the potential loss of their jobs. "Our general manager actually stated that every person is replaceable, and that the work they do, anyone can do," explained DePinto. "I think her insensitivity comes from her background, where employees are expected to fall in line when a directive was given. It doesn't work that way in our company."

As a result of the senior leader's comments, the emotional tone concerning the transition change program has turned very negative. DePinto is concerned that employees in both North America and Europe will begin to leave the company, which can put the entire transition strategy at risk. According to DePinto, "If we lose people in the existing service centers before the services transition to the new global service center, the entire transition will fail. Our senior manager has created significant risk for us and I really don't want to be the one trying to hold the transition together when it begins to fall apart."

This example demonstrates the critical need for strong senior management support and hands-on involvement for all global transition efforts while an organization is going global (which may take many years to accomplish).

Global Execution Challenges

The disciplines of international business management and leadership have become quite complicated and complex. Images of international trade and business from before the Industrial Revolution seem easy compared to today's global markets and economy. Jarred Mills, one of the many global managers that we spoke with during the research for this book told us that the expanse of globalization in recent decades has indeed complicated work. Specifically, he said, "In the beginning, it was easy, or at least easier. There was just one team, one site, and one manager. Then the 'Global Strategy' was handed down from our executive team. The strategy aimed to create better products, faster, and cheaper. We started using global teams as part of this strategy. As this new strategy unfurled, facing new complications and complexities became routine."

Mills is responsible for a team of engineers located in four U.S. states including Oregon, California, Texas, and New York, as well as locations in Switzerland, Poland, and India. "To say there have been significant challenges [with executing the global strategy] is a vast understatement," states Mills. The challenges that Mills faces are ubiquitous for all managers of globally-distributed teams and include communication, continual change, conflict resolution, motivating a diverse workforce, and the more obvious such as time zone mapping, recognizing and planning to work around cultural- and faith-based holidays, and other competing dimensions of work, life, and society. Mills broadly categorizes these challenges as differences. "The differences from California to Texas alone are enough to drive a manager crazy," he said. He went on to explain, "The [cultural] challenge is quite significant because I must be culturally sensitive myself to the team that I am trying to coach into being culturally sensitive. This challenge is magnified when multiple countries are involved."

Cultural difference is not only a potential global execution barrier for senior managers of an enterprise to resolve, cultural sensitivity is also a constant challenge for any project or program team leader leading a global team. Senior managers, working with their global team leaders should address this as part of the senior management-led strategy for addressing and managing across cultures. However, there are additional common execution challenges that each project or program team leader will most likely face when leading global teams. The most significant of these challenges that the global team leader must learn to overcome are the following:

1. Communication challenges;

2. Managing across time zones; and

3. Leading a highly distributed team.

Communication challenges

Communication is a common challenge for leaders of globally-distributed teams. It is said that the world language is broken English. Although English is spoken around the globe, it is done so as a second, third, or even fourth language for most people. But, understanding this challenge starts with recognizing that communication is more than just language. Communication is a challenge because of frequent misunderstandings when questions, responses, and requests are not well communicated or fully understood between the participants. When people do not understand one another, problems flourish.

According to Darrin Clark, a global manager responsible for 54 distributors worldwide, the challenge of global team communication is akin to the childhood game of "telephone," but on a global scale. "You tell somebody something, they pass the information to somebody else, and by the time it gets to the person that does the work – who of course is the person who needs the accurate information the most – they get a completely different message." Another member of the research sample, Kris Knopf, concurred, stating "The value of communication cannot be underestimated. From my experience working across four countries, this is a constant work in process. What I have learned is that a daily phone call and email does not constitute good communication."

With traditional co-located teams, it is common for project or program team members to participate in both formal and informal team meetings. Formal meetings are those held at a day and time broadcasted to team members in advance, with a set agenda, and pre-determined duration. Informal team meetings are those that take place arbitrarily, have no set agenda, no meeting length, and no formal invitations necessarily issued to all members of the development team ahead of the meeting time. They quite literally can be conversations that take place in the hallway or over lunch.[11]

We find that informal meetings are just as important (or potentially more so) than formal meetings for members of a development team. These meetings are where much of the cross-functional communication occurs that helps to stitch together the work that spans organizational boundaries. Unfortunately, in a globally-distributed team, these informal meetings and communications are limited to members located within the same geographical area and physical location within that area. As a result, informal meetings between team members rarely happen and much of the lower-level cross-functional and cross-organization communication fails to take place.

Becky Christopher, a manager of an international software company's program management office explained the challenge of communicating with a globally-distributed team: "As a global leader and team member, I am unable to wander down the hall to resolve challenges, momentarily brainstorm or ask for ideas from someone who has a similar project." This example highlights the integrated nature of this challenge with the obstacle of time zones and emphasizes the transaction time associated with what can be a simple exchange. "It can often take over twenty-four hours to resolve a simple question through email. When I send a question to a person in another country, perhaps twelve or twenty-four hours later I get a clarifying question, which is addressed by email a day later, just to find out that not all of the information is in the email that addresses my request. So, I then ask the question differently – via email, of course. I finally get the data needed to address the question." It can take several days to get accurate data to and from a globally-distributed team as compared to several hours, or even minutes, with a co-located team.

The challenge for the global project or program team leader then becomes one of finding a way to effectively compensate for the lack of informal meetings. This may mean that more formal meetings need to be set up and facilitated to promote the cross-functional and cross-organizational communication required. The challenge then becomes one of promoting more formal communication meetings for the team without leading them to a 'death by meeting.'

Managing Across Time Zones

The world is divided into 24 standard time zones with 40 factural time zones.[12] Early ideals of globalization highlighted the value of 24-hour per day work cycles. The thought was that products, as an example, could be originally designed in North America, developed in the Far East, tested in the Middle East, modified in Western Europe, and then iterated again in North America. Theoretically, this made for a 24-hour seamless work cycle. As described in the challenge of communication, little is actually realized from such theoretical cycles. A 24-hour work cycle does not equate into 24-hours of productive work. The once idealized notion of *'work while we sleep'* is realized most often as *'wait while we sleep'* because of the lack of smooth transitions between work teams around the globe trying to take advantage of time.

An additional realization of a 24-hour clock is that the global team experiences 12-hour variances in business operations, thus ensuring early morning and late evening team meetings and gatherings. It is easy to work across time zone variances in your own country. For example, when colleagues work together in North America, an early morning meeting is still morning in each of the locations. The time difference between New York and Los Angeles is three hours. So, an 8:00 AM meeting for a team in Los Angeles is an 11:00 AM meeting for the team a New York.

To include team members from India, however, becomes a greater challenge. Consider the variance between New York and Bangalore. One location will be in the morning and the other the evening. There is another challenging wrinkle of concern. These locations do not have a full hour variance, but rather a half hour variance. The difference in time is 10 ½ hours. Thus, an 11:00 AM meeting in New York is 9:30 PM in Bangalore. These two locations can squeeze a meeting together in roughly the same work day if the meeting starts at 7:00 AM New York time, which would be 5:30 PM in Bangalore. This meeting would be problematic, however, if we add the team from Los Angeles – where it is 4:00 AM on the west coast of North America. Such is the challenge currently facing our global project and program teams.

Stephanie Moraine, an infrastructure manager responsible for twenty-three country locations in Europe noted the repercussions from global team endeavors. "Global teams have the potential to create work-life balance issues – or work-life imbalance – due to team meetings inevitably being late nights and early mornings. This is especially true when teams span Europe, China, the U.S., and Russia – members from the team will be working through breakfast, lunch, and dinner."

Another repercussion is perceived in-group favoritism due to convenience. A member from our research sample confessed that "When you have global responsibility you tend to spend your time in the regions that may not necessarily need help, but rather that are the most convenient. I spend more time with Europe than I do the other regions because it is easier to get up early and check in with them. The Pacific Rim comes online in the evening and it is difficult to have a personal life and do conference calls between 6 PM and 10 PM. Because of this I am more detached from the Pacific Rim, which creates some serious challenges."

Time zone distribution will challenge project and program team leaders as long as our companies continue to develop their products and services in a highly-distributed global manner. The comments from members of our research sample remind us that the challenge then becomes one of effective leadership by the project or program team leader in ensuring that global best practices in managing time zone differences and virtual meetings are consistently followed and adjusted periodically to resolve problems as they arise.

Leading the Distributed Team

Globalization creates increased pressure on the team leader. As the world becomes a more integrated place, the demand for leaders as integrators will increase. Jarred Mills concluded that "Globalization will intensify and therefore our work as managers and leaders will only get harder and more complex." Leaders responsible for globally-distributed teams will be pressured to know about global and local economic situations, be politically savvy, legally adept, and culturally sensitive, be organizationally grounded in human resource management and team development skills, and be experts in their content area.

Effectiveness hinges on a new way of thinking. Top-down control is not a viable model in an interdependent global society.

Fewer layers are necessary. Moreover, a global strategy must be one that is visionary in its abstraction yet locally adaptive in its action. If each individual involved in executing the global strategy cannot see and understand their role in helping to achieve the end-state vision, then the global strategy will be challenged to succeed.

Opportunities abound for individuals within organizations who can effectively transform themselves and help assimilate diverse groups of people toward a common goal. This will require the global team leader to quickly and effectively establish trust and respect from and among the team. There is no greater asset than trust in and from your teammates when they are scattered across the globe, and there are fewer challenges harder to overcome than establishing a high level of trust in a highly-distributed, culturally-diverse team.

One of the biggest mistakes a global team leader can make is to underestimate the power of team trust. Creating trust requires a more conscious and planned effort on the part of the global project or program team leader. They need to take total responsibility for their actions as well as the actions and results of their teams.[13]

Looking Ahead

In this chapter, we evaluated the effects of misalignment of global strategy and the corresponding execution of that strategy. We provided an analysis of the barriers and challenges, the results of which reveals the two primary themes upon which the next two chapters are built: first, senior leaders within an organization must create an organizational environment that enables successful global team execution; and second, project and program team leaders who are being asked to execute in a global environment must have the specialized knowledge, skills, and tools to successfully shift from domestic team execution to global team execution.

Understanding what are the most common barriers and challenges to successful global execution, and who within the organization should be responsible for resolving them is the first step toward more effective global performance; learning how to overcome them is the more difficult step. Fortunately, globalization leaders have encountered and overcome many of these barriers and challenges, and have established a number of best practices and behaviors for the rest of us. The next chapter describes many of these best practices and behaviors in detail.

CHAPTER THREE

Aligning Global Strategy and Execution

"Strategy consists of meaningless words if it cannot be effectively executed."
- Unknown

When senior managers of global companies are asked if they are responsible and accountable for creating and implementing the globalization strategy for their firms, unanimous affirmation is received that they do in fact own that responsibility. When the same senior managers are asked if they are responsible and accountable for execution of the globalization strategy, answers are generally mixed. Some senior leaders fully believe they are responsible for execution success, while others believe the responsibility lies with their middle managers and their project or program team leaders.[1]

This parallels the difference in senior management philosophies within global companies. Senior managers of leading global enterprises believe they are responsible and accountable for setting the globalization strategy for their companies and for ensuring the necessary organizational changes and behaviors are driven across the enterprise to enable the successful execution of the strategy by their global project and program teams.

By contrast, there is significant evidence that the frustrations and challenges being encountered by global project and program teams within global-follower companies are due in large part to the failure of the senior managers within these companies to lead in the removal of the global execution barriers discussed in Chapter Two. In order for the global project and program teams to begin operating more effectively within a highly-distributed global environment, senior managers must step beyond setting globalization strategy and become personally engaged in enabling global project or program execution success.

Chapter Three focuses on the senior leaders of the organization, whose responsibility it is to create a global execution environment in which their project teams can successfully operate. Specifically, we cover the organizational and behavioral changes that senior leaders within a global company must drive in order to eliminate, or at least diminish, the common global execution barriers that prevent successful product and service development in a global environment.

Putting Skin in the Game

In the previous chapter, we presented the assertion that a series of structural, operational, and behavioral changes have to take place to move an enterprise from local success to global success. These changes are the responsibility of the senior managers of the enterprise and are necessary to avoid or overcome the most common and significant global execution barriers that prevent a company from effectively operating in a global environment. Before we detail the best practices that leading global companies use to effectively resolve the global execution barriers, let us revisit the senior manager's responsibilities in addressing the barriers.

Senior managers of global product and service development companies need to establish the right structures and performance measures to foster a highly-collaborative and distributed development model. The managers must drive all changes necessary to de-emphasize strong organizational silos that create collaborative barriers, and must also change individual performance measures and rewards for their middle managers and team leaders to those based upon achievement of team goals primarily, and individual goals secondarily.

As a company expands its product and service development activities across the globe, it rapidly becomes a multi-cultural entity. Senior managers must work to blend national, functional, and organizational cultural aspects of the organization and its workforce. Doing so aligns the enterprise to a common vision and set of goals.

Global product and service development requires a development model that facilitates a high degree of collaboration, synchronization, communication, and integration. Senior managers of global organizations must evaluate their current development model to determine if it provides that level of facilitation, and if needed, drive changes toward a development model that is more collaborative in nature.

Senior managers must ensure that the role of their global project and program team leaders is appropriately defined to meet the more broad-based and comprehensive requirements to succeed in a global environment. Along with appropriate role definition, senior managers of an organization must ensure that the project and program team leaders possess the requisite knowledge, skills, and experience to lead a global team, or acquire the appropriate resources outside the firm. This also includes providing the team leaders with the empowerment – responsibility and authority – along with senior management support – to effectively manage across the functions within an enterprise.

Lastly, all global transition change management efforts must be driven from the top of the organization. This requires senior leaders to advocate for the need and the value of the change, to strongly champion the transition project teams, to set expectations throughout the company that all members of the organization incorporate the change, and to hold people accountable for doing their part to transition the organization into a global leader.

Changing Organizational Structures for Global Execution

Senior leaders within leading global companies have had to change their fundamental thinking about how their organizations are structured. Instead of thinking about departments and functional silos, they have come to view their organizations as flexible, horizontal networks of resources. Senior managers within companies that are recently embarking on the globalization path or those struggling with global execution may have to evaluate how their organizations are structured.

This change in thinking has been driven by the realization that global execution success is anchored on four vital success factors related to the structures of an organization:

1. The global project or program team leaders must have direct access to the senior leadership of the organization;

2. Global execution is focused on management of the horizontal interfaces and dependencies across the organization;

3. All global team members need to have access to important technical and business information; and

4. Decision-making power must shift from the top of the organization to the global teams within well-defined boundaries.[2]

Traditional, hierarchical organization structures become a direct barrier to these four success factors.

To ensure alignment between a firm's globalization strategy and its global execution output, the senior managers and global project and program team leaders must have direct access to one another. They must, in fact, work together as a leadership team. Traditional hierarchical organization structures normally prevent this from occurring due to the horizontal layers that exist between the senior executives and the project or program team leaders.

The greater the number of layers between the global project and program team leaders and top-level management, the greater the probability of misalignment between strategic goals and execution output. This is a result of the lack of direct communication between executives and global team leaders, as well as the skewing and diluting of communication as it is passed between the layers of the organization.

Another phenomenon of the hierarchical organization is agency theory. Agency occurs when a misalignment of goals between a manager (the "principal") and an employee (the "agent") develops. This phenomenon is prevalent in organizations with strong functional silos. Agency theory occurs when functional managers design goals that provide the greatest benefit for their functional organization, with the strategic goals of the company being a secondary consideration.[3] If the global project or program team leaders are reporting directly to the functional managers, and do not have direct access to senior managers, the result of agency is that the global team many times drives to achieve the goals of the functional organization, and not the goals of the overall business.[4]

Since the project and program team leaders within a hierarchical structure are most times contained within a functional silo, it is very difficult for them to reach across the organization and drive cross-discipline and cross-geography collaboration in a global environment. A hierarchical structure can force project or program decisions to move beyond the project or program team leader to the functional managers of the organization. In the case where a decision crosses organizational boundaries, the decision must move to the appropriate organizational function and down the chain of command within a silo. This obviously becomes a very ineffective and inefficient mode of decision making in a global setting due to the time it takes to reach a decision.

The same structural barriers exist when it comes to accessing technical and business information. Team members normally have access to the functional-specific data and information contained within their organizational silo; however, they can seldom directly access data and information contained within another functional silo. They therefore have to resort to the same chain of command approval path as described above and will realize the same result – delayed or forbidden access to critical data and information.

Finally, hierarchical structures are power driven by design, with those at the top of the organization possessing the most positional power. The project or program team leader possesses very little positional power, which creates an execution barrier that makes it very difficult for the team leaders to effectively lead and influence a broadly-distributed global team. This normally leaves the functional managers who are more disconnected from the project or program, and who are not familiar with the daily execution activities, in charge of the project or program decisions.

Flattening the Organization

The leading global companies have much flatter organizational structures as compared to global followers. This is especially true in high-technology industries in which companies have been operating in a global environment for several decades.[5]

Figure 3-1 illustrates a lattice or matrix organizational structure that is commonly used in successful global enterprises. The multiple layers present in the hierarchical organizational structure are collapsed in the matrix structure.

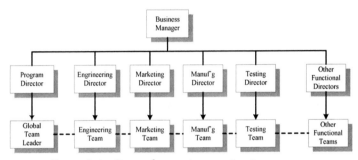

Figure 3-1: Example matrix organization structure

In a matrix structure, the project or program team leaders have easy access to the top management of the organization. This creates a direct communication channel and collaborative arrangement between the senior leaders and the project or program team leaders. This is a critical element in aligning globalization strategy to global execution outcomes because it fosters communication, which leads to an aligned community.

A matrix structure also results in a de-emphasis of functional silos, with the various organizations now owning a shared responsibility for project or program success. Each of the functional managers must invest in the project or program by providing resources (people, money, equipment, or materials). The return on investment is dependent upon the successful achievement of the project or program business goals. Therefore, participation in cross-organization collaboration is in their best interests.

Also of critical importance for success in a highly distributed environment is that decision-making power shifts to the project or program team leader. When a flat organization structure is instituted, the balance of power moves away from the functional managers and to the global project or program team leaders. This gives the global project team leaders greater decision-making power and more degrees of freedom to operate.6 Transfer of power enables the global team leader to distribute the decision-making power to the local level where people with the best information and most knowledge about a specific project or program situation exist.

Finally, a flat organization structure allows the project or program team leader to execute his or her primary role in leading the global team – integration of the work activities and work output of the highly-distributed team. The flat organizational structure enables the global project or program team leader to work horizontally across the functional disciplines of the enterprise. In doing so, he or she drives the creation of the holistic solution that directly contributes to the realization of the firm's globalization strategy.

Adopting the Right Development Model

As described in Chapter Two, many product and service development models break down when applied in a global environment due to the highly-distributed nature of the team and of the work. The senior leaders of an organization need to be willing to re-evaluate the effectiveness of their current development model as they move into the global environment. Most importantly, they must be willing to drive change to a new development model if it is deemed necessary and beneficial.

There is a set of core criteria for a development model that must be met when product or service development is performed across the globe. First, the development model must be flexible in nature, in that it must not matter where development resources are located, but that the work output of the distributed workforce is effectively integrated into a holistic solution in the end.

Second, a global development model must establish continual alignment of the execution output to the business goals of the organization for which the development effort was initiated. It is easy for resources that are separated by time, distance, and organizational function to forget the overriding business reasons for which they are expending personal effort.

Third, a global development model must provide a common cadence for which the work of the team is synchronized over the development lifecycle. Even though the development team members are highly distributed over geographic boundaries and time zones, their work is highly interdependent; therefore, they need to be working toward common delivery milestones, utilizing common methodologies and processes, and sharing common tools to stay in synchronization over time. Failure to do so leads to confusion and chaos across the global team.

Lastly, a global development model must emphasize cross-organization collaboration and de-emphasize the functional silos within an organization. Management of a global development effort, therefore, must focus on management of the interdependencies between the functions involved instead of focusing solely on the output associated with any of the functions.

There are multiple development models that are utilized to manage global product and service development efforts. The program-based development model, more commonly known as the program management model was created decades ago to manage highly-distributed development efforts and continues to be effective for managing global product and service development efforts. In a recent study by BusinessWeek that looked at best practices for achieving globally-distributed product development success, program management was identified as the most effective means for overcoming global product development challenges by leading global companies.[7] A study conducted in 2008 by the American Productivity and Quality Center on distributed collaboration echoed this finding.[8]

The Basis of Program Management

Many product and service development efforts today are quite complex in nature, especially as compared to those from just a decade ago. Development complexity manifests itself in several ways including: the ability to integrate multiple technologies to meet customer desires is becoming increasingly challenging; the processes used to assemble the solutions are more complex; and the development of the solution in a global environment where a multi-discipline, multi-company and multi-geographical approach stretches the abilities of many organizations.

Of course, management of complex development efforts is not new. Program management was initiated in the 1950s as a way to manage highly-complex development efforts in the defense and aerospace industries. What is new today is that development of products and services is commonly performed in a global environment – therefore introducing the complexity associated with distributed development.

Historically, the most effective approach for developing distributed solutions has been to employ systems engineering techniques. A system is defined as *a combination of parts that function as an integrated whole*.[9] Systems concepts can be used to describe a program in a similar manner. The projects that make up a program become the subsystems as illustrated in Figure 3-2. The arrows in this illustration represent the interdependencies between the projects – primarily deliverables from one project passed to another project. The tight knit of interdependencies between projects demonstrates that the success of the program is dependent upon the success of each of the projects. Said another way, if any one of the projects fail, the entire program will fail.

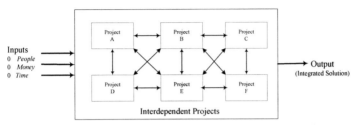

Figure: 3-2: Systems concepts applied to program management

Global product and service development companies have recognized that the program management development model can be extended to successfully organize and manage their highly-distributed teams. The teams are organized into multiple projects, corresponding to the element of the product or service they are developing, and then collectively managed within a single program.

The key to successful development under a program-based model is to use a top-down approach which begins with a conceptual design of the final product or service being developed: begin with the end solution in mind. The concept can then be disaggregated into pieces and formed into projects, distributed across the globe to the appropriate specialists to develop, and then re-integrated into a physical solution.

To demonstrate the top-down approach of defining a program in a global environment, we use a simple example of the development of a personal computer product (see Figure 3-3). The left side of the diagram represents the conceptual idea of what the final solution will be – the personal computer.

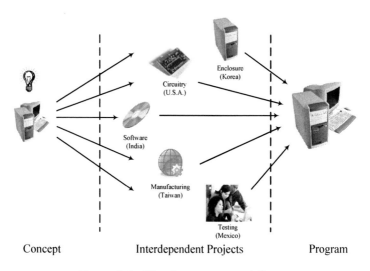

Concept   Interdependent Projects   Program

Figure 3-3: Top-down program definition

From the concept of the final 'system,' the projects within the program can be defined by the various elements to be developed. In this simple case, the projects consist of enclosure development, circuit board development, software development, product manufacturing, and testing. Each project is led by a project manager, and the work of each project team is focused and tactical: to plan, develop, and deliver its respective element of the solution to the other members of the program team.[10]

With the projects defined, the work to develop the output of each project can be distributed across the globe as it makes sense. In this example, the enclosure development is performed by the project team in Korea, the circuit board development is completed in the United States, the software is developed in India, the product is manufactured in Taiwan, and testing is performed in Mexico.

To ensure that the work of each project team is occurring in a coordinated and collaborative manner, and that the work is synchronized over time, the projects are managed within a single program and led by a global program manager. The role of the program manager is to ensure that the project elements are developed synchronously and integrated into a holistic solution, and that the distributed team remains focused on the achievement of the business results for which the product or service development effort was initiated.

Aligning Strategy and Execution

As illustrated in Figure 3-4, the global program manager assumes ownership for the strategic business goals for which the program is conceived to deliver. Through the process of leading the global development program, the program manager ensures that all distributed project teams are focused upon and working in concert to achieve the business goals.

Figure 3-4: Aligning execution output to business strategy

Within the program management development model, execution output is linked to business strategy through the integration of the deliverables and work flows of multiple interdependent projects. The project deliverables are integrated at the program level into a solution that then becomes the means to achieve the strategic business goals.

Horizontal Collaboration

In a business model where the work elements of a global product or service development team can be digitized, disaggregated, distributed across the globe, modified, and reintegrated into a holistic solution, a development model that facilitates a high degree of horizontal team collaboration is necessary.[11] Within a program-based development model, both the program manager and the respective project managers are responsible for the success of the program and product or service under development, but they operate in differing dimensions.

This concept, as illustrated in Figure 3-5, is a core differentiator of the program management development model.[12] Shown in the figure is a simple example of the five functional elements that are involved in the personal computer development program discussed previously: circuit board development, enclosure development, software development, manufacturing, and testing.

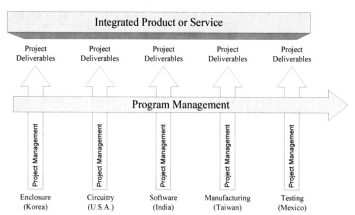

Figure 3-5: The collaborative nature of program management

Both the vertical and horizontal elements involved in the management of a program are clearly evident in the figure. First, let us look at the *vertical* or project element. The project teams, which consist of functional specialists located in various locations across the globe, are responsible for the development and delivery of their respective piece of the product or service under development. They are held accountable for the plans, schedules, risk mitigation strategies, quality levels, and deliverables as they pertain to their respective projects.

The work of the program manager cuts across the functional project teams, therefore managing the *horizontal* dimension of the program. The program manager drives the cross-discipline, cross-organization collaboration needed to create an integrated solution. Within a common program lifecycle framework, the program manager synchronizes the work of the project teams as they develop their respective pieces of the whole solution. Use of a common framework ensures that the work of the highly-distributed global program team is being performed on a common cadence that facilitates the synchronization and integration of work output.

Program Team Structures

A change in the way a firm organizes its development team structure may also be necessary to ensure maximum collaboration is occurring in a global development model. Like hierarchical organization structures, hierarchical team structures also stifle cross-team collaboration and communication. The program team structure therefore must be flattened to create a network of specialists and enable the integration of work flow and work output across the distributed team. Communication and collaboration should occur horizontally across the team, not vertically through a team hierarchy.

The program core team structure is the most common team structure found in global companies that utilize a program-based model (see Figure 3-6).[13] The global core team is the cross-discipline leadership and decision-making body of the program which is responsible for ensuring that both the program and business goals are achieved.[14]

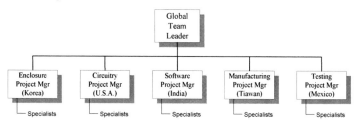

Figure 3-6: The global core team structure

The global core team consists of the team leaders who represent the organizational functions and provide leadership for the delivery of their function's element of the product or service under development.[15] The core team must become a very cohesive team that is willing to share responsibility for the success of the overall program. As Figure 3-6 illustrates, the project specialists within each of the geographies are only two levels removed from the global team leader.

The global core team structure is highly integrated, meaning there is joint consideration of trade-offs, decisions, and problem resolution between members of the team. Coordination and communication within the core team occurs both horizontally and vertically. Figure 3-7 demonstrates the triangulation of collaboration and communication that takes place on a core team. Directions, decisions, and cross-team issue brokerage comes from the program manager. Cross-team communication and work coordination occurs between the project managers. Status, decision consultation, and issue escalation comes from project managers to the program manager.

Figure 3-7: Core team collaboration and communication triangulation

Each member of the core team must be committed to the success of the other members on the team. A primary responsibility of the global program manager is to build a trusting, cohesive core team and lead them to mutual success by way of program success.

Developing Global Team Leaders

Even with the right organizational and team structures in place and the right development model instituted, successful product and service development in a global model will be hampered if the people leading the global teams are not adequately skilled and are not given the responsibility and empowerment to succeed.

The senior managers of an organization need to support the creation of training and development programs to increase the skills and competencies of the people charged with leading their global product and service development efforts. Additionally, the senior leaders need to recognize that the team leader for a global product or service development effort should be wholly responsible and accountable for the intended business results and, as such, be given the empowerment needed to manage resources and make decisions appropriate for the level of responsibility. This new team leader role in essence serves as the proxy for senior management in delivering the business results for their specific development effort. The responsibility and accountability given to the project or program leader is initiated and consistently reinforced by the senior leaders of a company.

Global team leader skills and competencies

The level of responsibility and accountability granted to global project and program leaders clearly requires a skill set and level of competence that is much higher than that of the traditional project manager who is many times put into the role of leading a global product or service development team. Successful global team leadership demands a skill set that includes business and financial acumen, understanding of the products, services and customers served, and proven evidence that they possess the "hard" and "soft" skills of leadership necessary to effectively lead complex development efforts in a highly-distributed virtual team environment.

Figure 3-8 illustrates the core competency areas that a global team leader should possess, or work to acquire through personal development, in order to be most effective in leading a globally-distributed team. We provide full details of the various skills needed within each of the competency areas in Chapter Six, but a summary description of the competencies is provided below.

Figure 3-8: Global Team Leader Competency Model

Effective leadership abilities are foundational to the success of a global project or program team leader. Specifically, we are referring to team leadership competencies, the ability to lead the cross-organizational, cross-geographical, and cross-cultural team. The core leadership competencies of the global team leader fall in two general categories: general leadership skills that are extended to leading a highly-distributed and multi-cultural team; and specific global team leadership skills that when possessed by the team leader significantly raise the probability of success in the global environment.

Leading a virtual team effectively requires the global team leader to be able to think globally and present the big picture or vision to his or her team in order to effectively synthesize the work output from the various distributed team members. Additionally, the team leader must be adept at communication and have sufficient emotional intelligence skills to effectively obtain balance and optimization on many fronts that present the need for tradeoff decisions. He or she must possess sufficient technological competency to help select the right communication and collaboration technologies, and become proficient in utilizing them in leading the team. Finally, the global project or program team leader must become politically savvy, knowledgeable in the cultures represented on the team, and aware of cultural norms of the nations in which the team directly works.

The global team leader should also possess sufficient business acumen to appropriately manage the business aspects of the project or program and to understand the impact on the effort from the various international economies in which the team is involved. Business competencies include the ability to develop a comprehensive project or program business case that supports the company's objectives and strategies, the ability to manage within the business aspects of the company, and the ability to understand and analyze the related financial measures pertaining to the product or service under development.

With respect to customer or client understanding, at a minimum level, the global project or program team leader must understand the customer's or client's needs that are pertinent to the product or service under development. They must possess sufficient technical knowledge and capability to understand how the needs can be met by the development effort and to integrate the elements of the design and development into a successful solution for the customer or client.

Lastly, the global team leader should be well versed in the core product or service development processes of the firm as well as basic project management processes, methods, and tools to effectively manage the tactical elements of the global project or program. An important aspect of this core skill set is that of becoming proficient at possessing a solid working knowledge of the specific processes and practices of the company. Knowing how things get done, the policies and procedures that must be adhered to, who must be involved, and who can approve various aspects of the development effort are all critical.

Global project and program team leaders do not come to their roles fully proficient in all competency areas, of course. As previously noted, they need to be trained and grow into their role through accomplished experience. The senior managers of an organization must be willing to invest in the continuous development of their global team leaders. Global project and program team leaders cannot gain the necessary expertise by learning the skills in the classroom or from reading a book on the topic. They have to practice and improve over time. Leading global teams is a complex undertaking, and a considerable amount of time may be required to achieve the level of mastery needed to be an expert in the field.[16] Improvement comes with a history of successes and failures associated with actually leading global teams, and true evidence of competence comes from a track record of proven accomplishments.

Team Leader Empowerment

Once responsibility and accountability is vested in a project or program team leader, senior leaders within the organization must formally empower the global team leaders with the appropriate level of authority and decision power that is commensurate with their level of responsibility. This change in the organization power structure must be communicated by the senior managers to all vested managers and participants of the enterprise.

A global project or program team leader's ability to execute important responsibilities and tasks depends on access to critical resources and empowerment by senior management to act beyond their initial or traditional scope of authority.[17] This transfer of empowerment from senior management to the global team leader is critical to success. It is analogous to being the high octane fuel that drives the efficient and powerful engine. Without it, even a well trained and capable project or program team leader is significantly hampered and cannot exercise the appropriate authority and decision making to achieve successful horizontal collaboration across the broader organizational structure and physical sites.

According to Roger Lundberg, former Director of Chrysler Development System and Vehicle Engineering Operations for Chrysler, "one of the most critical aspects of successfully executing in a global environment is to ensure project leaders are adequately empowered to make key trade-off decisions." However, Lundberg also explained that empowerment is not automatically granted, it has to be earned. "At Chrysler, a program manager has to demonstrate leadership competence in order to fully earn empowerment rights."

To illustrate, let's look at a situation faced by Tami Hughes, a senior program team leader in a global electronics company. Hughes works in a group that develops and manufactures its products across multiple sites in Europe, the United States, and Asia. Hughes's role has been defined as being responsible for meeting or exceeding the cost, performance, and schedule objectives for a new product code-named Sparticus.

Hughes believes she is adequately trained to successfully perform this responsibility and has been leading the cross-functional, cross-geography team for the past twelve months. Even though Hughes leads the team, the marketing organization controls all decisions relative to defining and launching the new product. Additionally, the engineering organization controls the technical decisions relative to the new product and controls the allocation of engineering resources to the programs based upon the engineering management's understanding and interpretation of program priorities.

The Sparticus program is currently three months behind schedule due to resource constraints, primarily in the software development team. Hughes has discussed her team's resource shortage and schedule shortfall with the Software Design Manager, Tom Brock, encouraging him to free up additional resources to get Sparticus back on schedule. Brock has made it clear to Hughes that all software engineering resources are currently fully committed to other programs and cannot be freed up. A further frustration for Hughes is that in a recent meeting with Bob Frank, the General Manager for the business unit for which she works, he made it clear that she will be held fully responsible for achieving the committed product launch schedule.

What Hughes is experiencing is a misalignment between responsibility and empowerment to successfully lead the global product development team. While she has been given full responsibility to achieve the business results intended, Hughes has not been given the empowerment to control the resources she needs to make it happen.

This example hits at the heart of the team leader empowerment challenge, all of which, as we pointed out earlier, are directly in the power of senior management to rectify. First and foremost, business and program priorities must be set by senior management and senior management alone. This should dictate how project and program team leaders and functional managers operate. When a conflict on resources arises between a team leader and a functional manager, for example, senior management must understand and accept their direct responsibility to intervene in these disputes so that the expected project priorities needed to achieve their business results are being followed.

Senior management has the ability to empower their project and program team leaders to be fully responsible for the business and operational results of their respective development efforts from initiation to launch. Within the decision boundaries agreed to between senior management and the team leader, the team leader should be empowered to make the necessary decisions on his or her development effort and correspondingly are held totally accountable to deliver results. This also includes the negotiation and commitment of resources from all functional disciplines, sites and other vested parties participating in the development effort.

Driving Global Transition

As we established earlier, going global normally requires significant change within an organization. Since each organization is unique, the specifics and extent of organizational change will also be unique for every enterprise. But commonly, the organizational changes necessary to make a globalization strategy successful are significant and can require months or years of effort to achieve.

Many senior leaders who set their enterprises on the globalization journey either underestimate or don't understand the amount of change that may be required. As well, they often don't realize that it is crucial for success that they remain personally involved and committed through the transition process.

According to a recent study on global product and service development by the American Productivity and Quality Center, continuous senior management involvement in the global transition journey is a key differentiator between the firms succeeding in global product and service development, and those still struggling to make the transition.[18] In fact, it is more than direct senior management involvement that is necessary. The senior leaders within an organization must drive the transition changes as well as the expectations, behaviors, and rewards for the firm's global project and program teams.

The critical components of senior management's leadership through the global transition process are covered in this section. These include:

- Providing strong support for the transition efforts;

- Fulfilling their role in the global product and service development process; and

- Promoting cultural diversity.

Providing strong transition support

What does strong senior management support for organizational transition efforts involve? We think the best answer to this question comes from someone who is in the trenches of global transition and has not had strong senior leadership support for their program. Susan DePinto, who we introduced in Chapter Two, is leading a global transition program that will move financial services offered in North America and Europe to her company's newer service centers in South America and Asia. DePinto has experienced the result of weak senior management leadership and support for her transition program and provides an excellent perspective on what is needed from the senior leaders within any organization that is undergoing organizational change:

- Communicate, communicate, communicate. Senior leaders should get in front of the organization early and often once a decision is made to execute a transition.

- Bring employees on the same journey. Paint the full picture of why the strategy is needed, how the decision was made, and what the anticipated impacts to the organization will be.

- Connect with employees. Show empathy for employees, develop an understanding of how the transition will impact them, and allow them to voice their opinions.

- Be a strong champion for the transition change management teams. This involves communicating the value of the team's work, setting realistic success criteria for the teams, actively working to eliminate impediments and barriers to progress, and rewarding and celebrating success when the work is completed.

While DePinto offers sound advice for senior leaders of an organization undergoing change related to globalization, her advice also applies to any senior leader who's organization is undergoing any significant change.

Early and often communication is a necessary component to organizational change success. Often, senior managers just spring an organizational change decision on the employees of the organization and fail to share the details involved in why the decision was made and how it will impact the organization. As the realities of the change begin to unfold, employees within the organization will continue to have questions, will continue to experience anxiety, and will need an opportunity to have their questions and anxieties addressed by the senior leaders of the firm. In addition to the senior managers of an organization continually communicating to their employees, they must also set expectations that their second and third level managers communicate a consistent message to their direct employees.

This means that the message must first be crafted from the top and then passed through the organization in consistent fashion, format, and context.

As part of the communication process, the senior leaders of an enterprise must bring their employees with them on the globalization journey. This means they should give all employees adequate information to understand the business reasons behind the decision to globalize, how the various implementation options were evaluated and selected, how it is anticipated that the selected options will help achieve the globalization goals, and what changes to the organization will be required along with impacts to employees (both positive and negative as the situation dictates).

No amount of direct communication will prevent employees from becoming anxious about how the organizational change might impact them personally, whether the impact is real or imaginary. Anxiety prevention is not the goal however. Keeping the workforce focused, motivated, and willing to perform their best is the *real* goal. The simple act of listening to employee's anxieties and showing empathy will go a long way toward achieving this goal. A critical aspect of leader communication is listening. An employee, having been listened to by a leader, begins to develop trust in the leader. People can understand the need for change and the tactics behind implementing the change, but in the process they need to know that the senior leaders of the organization view them as human beings with human emotions. Failure to do this can set the organization up for many emotionally-driven behaviors that will be counter productive to the goals of the change.

Senior managers must stay involved with the various transition change management projects and project teams that are driving the tactical aspects of the global transition. All too often, senior leaders are involved in scoping and approving the transition efforts, but either delegate the senior leadership oversight of the efforts to someone lower in the organization or fail to ensure that the oversight is provided altogether. To gain maximum probability of success, senior managers must be willing to stay engaged with the transition teams throughout the transition lifecycle.

This involvement can have many aspects – from ratification of all critical transition project decisions, to removal of obstacles, impediments and risks encountered by the teams, to keeping tension in the environment by setting realistic success measures and holding the teams accountable to achieve them. Additionally, the involvement may include promoting the need for the change that the teams are driving as well as the end state they are trying to achieve and continued cheerleading to keep the teams motivated when the transition effort meets resistance as it is being implemented.

Senior Management Role in the Development Process

As global product and service development teams are chartered and begin performing their duties on an on-going basis, it is important that the senior leaders of the enterprise have a visible and active role in the development process. In addition to providing senior level guidance to the teams, senior management involvement makes a statement that the success of the development effort is important enough for them to be personally involved.

Direct personal involvement on the part of senior managers is especially important during the early stages of transition from performing teamwork in a local environment to performing that work in a globally-distributed environment. The senior leaders must help to ensure that the development projects or programs are scoped appropriately for the skill level of the team; that the organizational structure is supporting the high degree of collaboration required; that the teams are structured in a way that promotes cross-organizational communication and collaboration; that the appropriate decisions are being made and risk is being managed at the team level; that the correct set of success criteria is defined and is being used to guide decisions; and that the key stakeholders of the project or program are fulfilling their roles and responsibilities as required to ensure that the global project or program is successful.

At a minimum, senior managers need to be involved in all critical decision points within the global project or program such as important business approval meetings and milestone checkpoints. During this direct involvement with the global teams, it is important for senior leaders to show that they are holding the global project or program team leader and his or her team accountable for the success of the development effort, that they are empowering the team to manage the effort appropriately, and are willing to be personally involved in removing any barriers or impediments to the team's success.

This level of involvement on the part of senior managers is necessary to ensure that behaviors of everyone involved in the global project or program are transitioning. Behavioral change is by and far the most difficult aspect of transitioning from performing work in the traditional manner to doing work in a new way. Not only is driving behavioral change difficult, but also it is normally one of the key determinants of transition change success or failure. Only the senior managers of the organization can set the expectation that behaviors need to change and to hold people accountable to perform their work as expected. This is especially true in a transition to a global and highly-distributed product or service development model where new people are introduced, personal relationships are not yet strongly established, and work cannot be micromanaged.

As time passes, the level of direct involvement on the part of the senior managers of the organization should become less as the structural and process components become more familiar, people become more comfortable in their new roles, and behaviors change in a manner that the global product and service development efforts become more effective and efficient. It should be expected that overall efficiencies will most likely become worse before they return to the levels experienced in a domestic or co-located environment. However, it is the direct involvement by the senior managers of the enterprise that is the key factor determining the velocity at which efficiency returns.

Promoting Cultural Diversity

Going global will lead to many changes within an organization. One of the most significant changes that enterprises encounter is the cultural diversification of its workforce resulting from the acquisition of talent from other parts of the world. While cultural diversification has many advantages and benefits that we will discuss shortly, when an organization is in the midst of cultural transformation, tensions between members of the workforce can occur. If these tensions are left unchecked and unmanaged, they eventually lead to conflict between members of the organization.

Specific to global product and service development teams, cultural tensions and conflict can result in team members beginning to participate and collaborate less frequently. The effectiveness of any global project or program team depends largely on the effective participation of its members – where participation involves contribution of information, sharing of ideas, and involvement in the team decision process. Proper management of cultural diversity and intra-cultural interaction among global team members is therefore critical to effective team member participation and team success.

It is the role of the senior managers of an organization to re-vamp the cultural vision of the firm to embrace and fully benefit from the new cultural components that globalization produces. Realization of the new cultural vision begins with creating an environment that encourages global team member participation through embracing and promoting cultural diversity.

The value and benefits of cultural diversity are well understood by the leading global companies within all industries, as they have learned to use cultural diversity as a competitive advantage. Among the greatest benefits are where cultural diversity:

- Uncovers new perspectives for looking at both opportunities and problems;

- Taps knowledge and experiences that are different from the members of the 'home' country; and

- Generates innovative ideas, suggestions, and methods.

An additional benefit that is not stated as regularly as those above but is of equal importance is the retention of employees with languages other than English as their first language. Such employees are crucial to an organization's ability to service their international customers.

The senior managers within leading global companies focus their efforts on a set of activities that promote and champion diversity within their organizations. We present the short list of activities below as examples of best practices associated with cultural diversity promotion.

Creating a cultural diversity council. This council is best chaired by a highly-respected senior manager and is responsible for ensuring that employees learn to encourage and value the contributions and differences of employees from varying backgrounds. It is the role of the diversity council to set the diversity strategy for the organization and approve and shepherd the various cultural diversity programs.

Creating cultural diversity education and awareness programs. The education and awareness programs must be sponsored by the senior leaders of an organization to ensure employee participation in the programs. For example, education and awareness programs may include tutorials that focus on the following:

- Understanding the cultural biases of each team member and their impact on mutual perceptions;

- Understanding why certain behaviors and communication styles fail in some cultures;

- Identifying approaches to address cultural issues that may lead to team conflict; and

- Learning how to handle issues concerning team decision-making.

Of utmost importance is that, like all major transition change programs, the senior leaders stay involved in the planning and implementation of the education and awareness programs.

Creating easily-accessible job aides. This involves creating information on how to conduct business successfully with clients and colleagues from another country. IBM, widely recognized as a global leader, calls their version of this 'Shades of Blue.' Their job aids are available via the IBM intranet and provide information topics such as 'culture and globalization,' 'culture and business,' and 'diversity and multi-cultural management'. These job aids were designed to heighten awareness of each person's own cultural biases and increase their sensitivity to other cultures.

Using measures to drive behaviors. It is a well known fact that what gets measured, gets improved. This is because measurement drives accountability which drives behaviors. In order to evaluate the effectiveness of a firm's cultural diversity program and influence change in personal behavior, key measures such as employee retention rates, team satisfaction ratings, client feedback, and training participation should be put in place and consistently evaluated by the senior leaders. Based upon the results of the measures, adjustments in the cultural diversity programs should be implemented.

When employees become more aware of and comfortable working in a culturally-diverse organization, they will be more prepared to recognize and act on global opportunities and will be able to operate more effectively in a variety of cultural and business environments, whether travelling abroad or participating in a global project or program team.

Looking Ahead

It is the responsibility of the senior leaders of the organization to create a global execution environment in which their project or program teams can successfully operate. The most fundamental change that must take place to successfully align global strategy and execution across the company is to de-emphasize the functional silos that exist in so many companies, and align them with a horizontal management framework that supports the high level of collaboration required to raise the probability of success for global project and program teams. We described a systematic approach to managing global teams including a comprehensive product or service development model, a horizontally-based organizational structure and philosophy, and a cross-disciplined, highly-collaborative team led by a qualified and well-trained project or program team leader.

With the senior managers of an organization focusing on the structural, process, and behavioral components that enable effective global execution, the next chapter focuses on the role of the project and program team leaders in overcoming the various challenges that can prevent them from effectively leading in a global environment.

CHAPTER FOUR

Leading the Global Project Team

"Teamwork is neither 'good' nor 'desirable.' It is a fact."
- Peter F. Drucker

As pointed out in Chapter Two, successfully executing a global strategy is the shared responsibility of senior managers and global project and program team leaders. With senior managers attacking the organizational barriers to successful global execution, the global team leader's responsibilities lie in working to overcome the most common challenges to effectively leading a globally-distributed team.

Whether operating in a domestic or global environment, the project team leader is accountable for the team's performance and the quality of its output. All leaders must grapple with four essential issues while building and leading the project team: (1) establishing the team vision, goals and objectives; (2) defining the roles and responsibilities for each member of the team; (3) instituting the team norms and work procedures; and (4) managing personal relationships.[1]

Successfully leading a team through these issues is difficult enough with a domestic, co-located team. It becomes much more complicated in a global, highly-distributed team environment due to the time, distance, and cultural complexities that exist. This chapter explains the essential factors needed and best practices used to overcome these complexities and successfully lead the global team to achieve its goals.

A Comparison of Global Team Leadership Results

Perhaps the easiest way to "see" success in global team leadership is through the distinction of end results. Let us compare two similar cases with distinct outcomes. The similarity of the cases is their business sector – aerospace – which has long been associated with the use of global project teams. At first glance, the similarities between Project Airbus 380 and Project Boeing 777 are obvious. Both companies are in business to develop and manufacture commercial aircraft, and both Project 380 and Project 777 aimed to design and manufacture a new commercial aircraft using a globally-distributed team. That is about where the similarities end.

Project 380

Airbus, headquartered in Toulouse, France, evolved from a consortium of companies primarily located across Europe. The final Airbus 380 assembly is performed in France. Preassembly of many component parts is distributed around the globe. Of particular interest here is the preassembly of wiring harnesses, which is performed in Germany. Although all parts are made to exact specifications, the harnesses were originally specified using software that was not in compliance with the newer version of software used by other teams, including the final assembly team in France. This problem was not uncovered until final assembly.

The result? A significant delay in the final product roll-out and a multi-billion dollar cost overrun.[2]

Project 777

Boeing is headquartered in Seattle, Washington, USA with a value chain of designers, engineers, suppliers, manufacturers, and other contractors from around the globe. More than half the component parts of the Boeing 777 aircraft are manufactured outside the United States. The experienced global project leader understood the need for team openness and collaboration. The worldwide team was structured using open-team concepts thus allowing and encouraging cross-team collaboration. Functional silos were eliminated from this project, with engineering, design, and manufacturing teams all working together. All team members met face-to-face several times throughout the project. These gatherings helped to increase communication effectiveness and, importantly, cultural, social, and individual awareness of the team's purpose, goals, and norms. Relative to communication, it was expected that anyone with suggestions or perceived risks for the project would make them known. The result? The most successfully designed and manufactured plane in Boeing history. The plane met customer standards, requirements, and expectations, and was easier to fly and maintain than any commercial airplane to date.[3]

As pointed out previously, success and failure in the global environment hinges in a large part on the alignment between a firm's globalization strategy and the execution of that strategy. When a misalignment exists within a firm, even the most senior and experienced domestic project or program team leaders encounter significant challenges when they first move to a global team setting. This is predominantly due to the increased level of complexity associated with global development efforts created by the dispersion of the team across multiple geographies, time zones, and cultures.

As leading global companies have discovered, adequately preparing their project team leaders for the transition from leading in a domestic environment to leading in a global environment is a crucial element for global execution success. So what does it take to successfully lead a globally dispersed product or service development team? The remainder of this chapter answers that question by focusing on the critical aspects of successful global team leadership.

Team Leadership Basics Still Apply

Contrary to what some project and program team leaders have come to fear, the team leader does not need to employ a completely new set of practices and processes, or learn a new suite of skills and competencies to succeed in leading a global project or program team. The foundational elements of effective team leadership apply whether one is leading a domestic team that is co-located (at a single site) or a global team that is distributed across multiple sites and geographies. Applying the basics in a global project environment is complicated, however, due to the varying cultural backgrounds of global team members, physical separation of the team members by geographical location and distance, variation of work schedules caused by time zone differences, communication time delays, and miscommunication and conflict caused by language differences.

Success begins with proficiency in the basic principles of team leadership, and then understanding how to extend the leadership principles for a distributed team application. Over time, the basic leadership principles can be augmented with additional processes, tools, and skills to increase effectiveness given the cultural, distance, time, and communication challenges.

Creating a Common Purpose

Bringing a group of people together and assembling them as a team does not make them think and behave as a team. Members of a team must view their work in terms of we instead of me; meaning, we must work together toward a common purpose that is defined by a set of common and agreed-upon business and project goals. The team leader's job is to establish the common purpose and to inspire the team to work collaboratively to achieve the goals that define the purpose. It is the ability of the team leader to create a common vision and the team's willingness to adopt that vision that defines a group of people as a team.

In the global team environment, the need for a well-defined common purpose is amplified in order to establish a foundation from which to begin building team cohesion. A clearly-articulated common purpose is the global project team leader's most valuable tool for driving ambiguity out of the environment and to get team members to think in terms of team goals ahead of personal goals.

When a global project or program team is formed, the team usually has very little in common. At times, such as in the case of a merger or acquisition of companies, the team members may not have even worked together previously. Additionally, in a merger or acquisition case, the team members join the team with very idiosyncratic perspectives in the way they are thinking and behaving within their own cultural and functional norms, and with their own personal goals ahead of team goals. Without the establishment of a clearly-articulated common purpose, a large degree of ambiguity and lack of focus can exist within the global team environment.

A clearly-defined common purpose is instrumental in removing ambiguity and should answer four key questions: (1) what is the purpose of this team – the mission; (2) what does the end-state product or service look like – the vision; (3) what do we need to accomplish to get to the end state – the objectives;

and (4) how will our success be measured – the success factors. The job of the global team leader is to create answers to these four foundational questions with input from the team members and stakeholders. Answers should be simple, direct and free from jargon to overcome competing cultures and mindsets and address both corporate needs and local conditions regardless of the global geography. To do so is the first step toward removing ambiguity from the project or program and getting team members to think and behave collectively instead of individually.

A concept called the whole product has been used by both domestic and global team leaders to successfully establish a common vision for their project teams. The whole product is simply defined as *the integrated solution that fulfills the customers' expectations.*[4] Integrated is the key word in this definition. This word tells us that the customers' expectations cannot be fulfilled by any one specialist or set of specialists on the team. Rather, success comes when meeting customer expectations is a shared responsibility between the project team members, with their work tightly interwoven and driven toward the integrated customer solution.

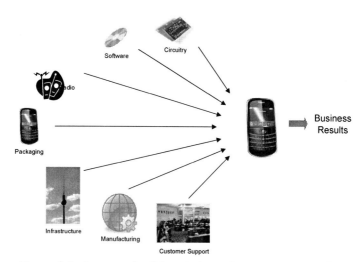

Figure 4-1: An example of the whole product concept in product development

96

Figure 4-1 illustrates in graphical format a simple example of the whole product concept in use on a product development project.

In this example, the development of a cellular phone, the whole product consists of all of the elements necessary to create the total solution for the customers of the company developing the product. Obviously, it consists of the various hardware, software, and wireless communication elements of the physical product, but it also consists of ancillary elements such as packaging, manufacturing, infrastructure enablement, marketing, and customer support. If any one of the primary elements of the whole product is missing, the product would fail to meet the customer and end user needs.

In a global team environment, the development of the elements would most likely be distributed to various team members and partner organizations across the globe. By creating and communicating the whole product description, each member of the global project team begins to see the holistic view of what the team is creating, and how their work output contributes to the whole.

The whole product, however, is merely the means to achieve the business results that are driving the need for the project. In the example above, the business results may include increased market segment share, higher profit margin, low product cost, accelerated time-to-market introduction, and advanced technology introduction. By including the anticipated business results in the description of the whole product, members of the global team begin to focus on success criteria that only can be achieved by the collective success of the team. The global team now has a common vision for performing its work in a collaborative manner.

Establishing Team Chemistry

A project or program team may consist of the top talent within an organization, but they will not reach a high level of performance without a certain bonding of spirit and purposefulness. It is this bonding, or team chemistry, that motivates team members to work together collaboratively for the common success of the team.

Of course, when a group of people form a team their personalities will not immediately gel. Acculturation of personalities, ideas, shared values, and goal alignment takes time as well as intentional effort (sometimes considerable effort) on the part of the project or program team leader.

People from a diverse set of backgrounds and experiences will bring different behaviors, routines, values, and ideas about the work of the team. The team leader must embrace this diversity of people on his or her team as individual members that make up a collective work unit, and act as a coach and role model for the rest of the team to help them embrace the value of diversity. What the team must learn is that there is great benefit to having differences in personality, values, opinions, and ideas working toward an optimal business solution. It is the result from this that enhances team decision making, problem solving, and goal attainment.

Establishing team chemistry on a global project or program team is considerably more complicated than on a domestic team. This is because of great cultural diversity and the increase in communication challenges due to language and time zone barriers brought about by the geographic distribution of the global team. As a result, it takes much more time and effort to blend national, organizational, and functional culture into a team culture where values, attitudes, and meanings come together from team members representing several nations.

Additionally, in a globally-dispersed team, it is more difficult to get to know people on a personal basis and to form close relationships due to the limited amount of ongoing face-to-face interaction. However, both the blending of culture and development of personal relationships are critical for the team to behave cohesively and consistently as a team instead of as individuals.

There are a number of things that successful global team leaders do to accelerate the establishment of team chemistry. These include establishing team norms, fostering social presence, using information-rich communication technologies, and celebrating team successes.

Establish team norms early in the formation of the team. With the team members, lead and facilitate a series of discussions on how the team will perform its work and conduct itself. In particular, focus on acceptable and unacceptable behaviors, meeting types and forums needed, communication preferences, how decisions will be made, and reporting methods, messaging, and frequency. Make sure to gain agreement on the norms and then set the expectation that the team behaves and acts in a way that upholds the norms.

Foster social presence. To prevent some members of the team from becoming invisible, make sure that all team members know one another and continue to foster connections. Initial introductions are critical, and must go beyond the usual statement of name, functional group, and one's understanding of the role one plays on the team. It's more effective to also ask each individual to describe his or her expertise and professional background, as well as something interesting and significant about his or her culture. Some global project and program managers have created simple social networking websites for their teams that provide member profiles.

Use information-rich technologies. Though not officially a technology, face-to-face interaction is far and away the most effective way to share information and facilitate team collaboration. One of the greatest outcomes of an initial face-to-face meeting is an acceleration of team chemistry building. Through both work and social interaction, the team will quickly begin to establish the foundational elements of team chemistry:

- The team learns how to work smoothly and unselfishly under the leadership of the global team leader and develop the ability to respect and get along with one another;

- Each team member begins to recognize the specific role he or she plays in contributing to the goals of the team;

- The team members begin to blend their individual efforts into the work of the other team members;

- Team members establish a mutual feeling of respect, loyalty, and empathy toward each other; and

- A sense of team identity begins to form.

Since regular face-to-face contact is not possible for a global team, the use of videoconferencing technologies will provide more interaction than voice-to-voice contact alone. At a minimum look to use videoconferencing or desktop videoconferencing technologies to allow team members to see one another while they communicate and collaborate.

Celebrate successes as a team. Making sure that the entire team participates in team celebrations goes a long way toward focusing team members on team accomplishments over individual accomplishments. The celebrations do not have to be large or even formal in nature to be appropriate and appreciated by the team members. Successful global team leaders look for additional opportunities to recognize team accomplishments throughout the duration of the project at key milestones, major events throughout the calendar, and even as surprises to the team to help manage project anxiety and pressures.

Building and Sustaining Trust

Trust within a team is the foundation of effective collaboration. For a team to reach its highest level of performance, much attention has to be paid to building trust between the team members and between the team and the leader, sponsors, and other stakeholders.

In his book *The 21 Irrefutable Laws of Leadership,* John Maxwell uses the analogy of building trust as either putting change into your pocket or paying it out.[5] Each time a project or program team leader forms a new team, he or she begins with a certain amount of change in his or her pocket, representing the inherent trust a person receives from his or her position as the team leader. As the project progresses, the team leader either continues to accumulate change in his or her pocket by building trust across the team, or finds that the pocket begins to empty when trust is depleting.

This analogy holds true for leaders of a global team as well, but there is a distinct difference. Because of geographic separation and cultural differences inherent in a global team, the project or program leader and team members may find their pockets void of change at the beginning of the global project – meaning, a global team may actually begin collaborating within an environment that is lacking trust. For domestic teams, some trust may exist based solely on social bonds that may be in place given their co-location and commonality in culture. Global teams do not have this social bond as a foundation of trust to build upon. Trust in a global environment is granted to those who demonstrate they are trustworthy, and therefore is built more upon consistent and proven performance by both the global team leader and the team members than by social bonds.

Table 4-1 lists the factors that both destroy and create trust on a project or program team. Obviously, the team leader is best served by acting upon the trust creators and avoiding the trust destroyers.

Trust Creators	Trust Destroyers
Act with integrity	Demonstrate inconsistency between words and actions
Communicate openly and honestly	Withhold information or support
Focus the team on shared goals	Put personal gain over team gain
Show respect to team members as equal partners	Engage in lies, sabotage, and scapegoating
Listen with an open mind	Listen with a closed mind

Table 4-1: Trust creators and destroyers

Building strong relationships between team members is also an important factor in enhancing and sustaining trust on a global project or program team, especially later in the life of the team. Because of geographic separation, creating and sustaining trust on a global team requires a more conscious and planned effort on the part of the project or program team leader. At a minimum, it will require the team leader to spend more time networking across geographic boundaries.

In many ways, the global team leaders are the glue that holds teams together. Establishing trust in themselves and between team members based on demonstrated trustworthiness can be a difficult task. They should begin by setting the expectation that the teams perform within the confines of the elements that demonstrate one is worthy of mutual trust:

- **Perform competently:** With the absence of personal relationships on a global team (especially at the beginning of the project), team members will be evaluating each other and the global team leader based upon how competent they believe a person is within their role on the team.

- **Act with integrity:** Global team members will closely watch and listen to determine whether other team members act in a manner that is consistent with what they say and within their stated values.

- **Follow through on commitments:** This means doing what you say you're going to do whether it is completing a project deliverable, sending an email when promised, or scheduling a meeting in a timely manner.

- **Display concern for the well-being of others:** People trust others who are perceived as responsive to the needs of others on the team and within the organization. Team members (and team leaders) who assess how their behaviors affect other team members most likely will be perceived as having more concern for others. On the contrary, those who appear to be less sensitive to others will be viewed as less trustworthy.

- **Behave consistently:** Members of a globally-dispersed team look for a higher level of consistency of behavior among their fellow team members as a way to drive out some of the ambiguity within a global team environment. Those who behave in a consistent manner are perceived as being more capable of being depended upon and therefore earn trust and confidence more readily from the other team members.

The global team leader must treat trust as his or her greatest asset and realize that it is important to consistently model the behaviors that exemplify competence, connection, and character in leading the team. The best global team leaders we have encountered realize the need to go beyond establishing expectations that the team demonstrate the trust building behaviors stated above. They also role model the behaviors on a daily basis by always standing behind and supporting their teams, never demonstrating favoritism, and accepting full accountability for the actions and results of their teams.

Demonstrating Personal Integrity

One of the surest ways to destroy trust on any team, domestic or global, is for the project or program team leader to demonstrate a lack of integrity. If one wants proof of the importance of leaders operating with integrity there are many stories in the press today that demonstrate the effects of lapses in integrity.

Team leaders who operate with integrity are described as those who behave ethically and honestly, have an unwavering commitment to their values and are willing to defend them, are authentic in that their thoughts and beliefs are displayed through their actions, and consistently demonstrate responsibility, accountability, and consistency.

For the global team leader, integrity is rooted in two foundational elements: values and vision. Values are what you stand for, and the team needs to see demonstrable proof of your values in action. Vision is a clear end state of where you are taking the team. For project or program team leaders, this involves establishing transparency in the project and business success criteria that tell the team what it takes to be successful in their mission.

Empowering the Team

With leadership, comes power. The most effective leaders are those who are willing to share their power with the members of their team who can make the most positive impact. As trust develops on a project or program team, the team leader should begin to delegate some of his or her power to other key leaders on the team through empowerment. Empowerment is the sharing of power from one person to another and granting them influence and authority to take responsibility and make decisions within their sphere of work. As explained previously, team empowerment means giving the project or program team members the responsibility and authority to make decisions at the local level. In their book The Power of Product Platforms, Marc Meyer and Alvin Lehnerd state that "there is no organizational sin more demoralizing to teams than lack of empowerment."[6]

As team members are granted greater empowerment, they will begin to act more on their own and rely less on the direction of the team leader. They will take on a greater sense of responsibility for their work output, become more comfortable with making decisions and solving problems on their own, begin to act proactively instead of reacting to change, and ultimately become more motivated to succeed.

For the project or program team leader, however, greater empowerment of the team members also means taking on greater risk. The more the team leader shares his or her power, the more he or she is betting that the team can and will perform on their own. The greater the empowerment, the less control the team leader maintains.

Team member empowerment is debatably more critical on a global team than a domestic team as it is an effective tool for quick and effective decision-making, where people closest to an issue are most suitable and able to evaluate the situation and decide the proper course of action. Slow and ineffective decision-making is a primary cause for schedule delays on global projects and programs.

For a global team leader, empowering the members of a project or program team is a very tricky undertaking due in large part to the cultural views of the team members and the time and geographic distance between the leader and members. It is further complicated when a high level of trust has not yet been established on a team and when a team is not fully aligned around a common purpose and set of goals.

Therefore, team member empowerment on a global project is more risky than on a domestic project, especially if full team alignment has not been established. Empowerment on a global team, therefore, must be granted cautiously over time. As a senior program manager from a major aerospace company told us, "Empowerment is something that builds over time through gaining the confidence of the team." He also pointed out that there needs to be empowerment boundaries, because as he put it, "one big screw-up on the part of someone wipes out ten 'attaboys'."

The most powerful tools for a global team leader to use in establishing effective team empowerment are clearly defined deliverables, identified owners for each deliverable, and decision boundaries based upon success criteria associated with each deliverable. This requires a detailed level of planning and execution on the part of the project leader and team, but is necessary until performance capability is demonstrated consistently on the part of the project team. Greater empowerment, with wider boundaries, can be granted as time and trust increase during the life of a global project or program.

Driving Participation, Collaboration, and Integration

Organizational alignment is a key differentiator between global leaders and followers. Gone is the time when project team leadership is authority driven with work being performed through a series of directives. Today's era of project and program team leadership is a more diffused, collective, team-based leadership, where directives and decisions are participatory, collective, and democratic. Success of the team leader is dependent upon how well he or she facilitates the alignment of interests, work activities, and the collective outcome of the organizational parts.

Product and service solutions are now too complex to be developed by a single expert. It requires the integration of work from a team of specialists who focus on creating their piece of the whole solution; however, specialists do not by nature desire to work in a collaborative and participative manner. They would prefer to be left alone to create their piece of the solution and hand it off to someone else to integrate and use.

Unfortunately for the specialists, this type of development has been proven to be highly inefficient and ineffective, and has led to the need for collaborative cross-functional work teams. Surrounded by specialists, the role of the project team leader becomes one of initiating and driving continuous, cross-team collaboration. In order to build a team that collaborates effectively, the team leader must drive active participation by all team members. Without active participation of the team members, a high performance team does not exist.

When leading a global team, the leader has to work even harder to drive effective participation and collaboration between members who are separated by time and distance. This is due primarily to the fact that participation and collaboration – as well as integration of work output – has to be performed asynchronously and electronically.

The physical distance that separates global team members limits the amount of synchronous collaboration. Face-to-face meetings and discussions are limited. This causes time delays due to the additional iterations of communication and work that result from trying to collaborate electronically and at differing times. Relatively routine tasks such as scheduling a meeting can become complex when one person's work day begins while another is sitting down to dinner.[7]

Time differences and physical separation can also allow some of the more introverted members of a team to become 'lost in action'; meaning, their participation and collaboration on the team can become lost due to their innate personalities. Focused effort on the part of the global team leader to keep these people active and engaged is necessary.

Integration of work output also becomes more complicated in a global environment. Work is accomplished in a very fragmented manner on a global team, and it will remain fragmented unless integration of work between members is purposefully established and managed by the project team leader.

Effectively driving collaboration, participation, and integration of work output therefore requires both a change in behavior and change in some processes on the part of the global team leader and the team members. To first establish broad participation of team members, the team leader must focus on some critical behaviors. He or she must be willing to listen first, and not be someone who tells their team what he or she thinks first, and then asks for opinions. Rather, a more effective approach to increase member participation is for the team leader to ask for input and opinions first, facilitate a discussion as a team, and then share his or her own opinions.

By doing so, the global team leader is motivating the team through inclusion. Through deliberated provocation of opinion from the team, the team leader helps his or her team members become more comfortable with participating and sharing their opinions as time progresses.

It is also possible to drive participation and collaboration through the project reporting system. The team leader must first establish the process for reporting progress, issues, and risks. This includes determining what information to include in a report, at what level of detail, in what format, and how often to report. The team leader must enroll his or her team members in the process, and then hold them accountable for following the process.

For a highly-distributed team, it is essential to drive for commonality in content and format in order to reinforce the fact that the members are part of a team, and that the team needs to perform many things in a like manner. Figure 4-2 illustrates a simple one-page progress report that can be created for each sub-team on the project, or for each project on a program. Establishing common reporting templates for the team to use serves to de-emphasize individual behaviors that destroy team collaboration.

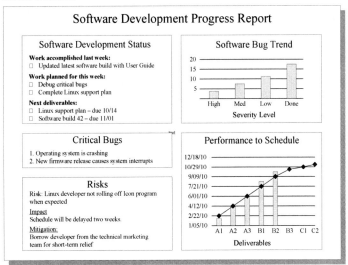

Figure 4-2: Sample one-page progress report

Effort must be made, and the expectation set by the global team leader, that progress reports are presented in the team environment, such as at a team meeting. Reporting frequency needs to be more often for a globally-distributed team than for a co-located team. The global team leader should establish a quick and frequent reporting cycle for the team – weekly at a minimum. Because of geographical separation of the team, lengthy time delays between progress reporting can allow work to drift off course and issues and risks to escalate out of control before the global team leader and other team members become aware of it.

Another effective approach for driving a high level of collaboration between members of a globally-distributed team is to organize the team's work in such a way that the team members are mutually dependent, and for them to realize that they are mutually dependent. An excellent process for establishing and managing the interdependencies on a global project or program is a process known as project or program mapping.

Co-located teams tend to manage their work by completion of tasks, whereas distributed teams more effectively (and visibly) manage their work by completion of deliverables. The project or program mapping process is used to identify the critical deliverables throughout the lifecycle for each sub-team on a project or for each project within a program, whichever the case may be. More importantly, the project or program map shows the cross-team interdependencies that exist between the members of the team.[8]

Figure 4-3 illustrates an example of a partial project map that shows the deliverables and cross-team interdependencies during a two-month period of the project. By following one of the deliverable chains, we can demonstrate how cross-team interdependency and collaboration is organized in this example. The power control SW is a deliverable generated by the software development team and delivered to the enclosure development

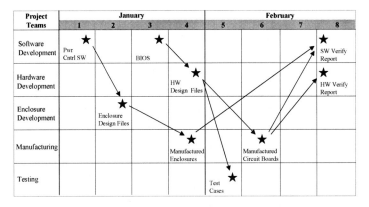

Project Teams	January				February			
	1	2	3	4	5	6	7	8
Software Development	★ Pwr Cntrl SW		★ BIOS					★ SW Verify Report
Hardware Development				★ HW Design Files				★ HW Verify Report
Enclosure Development		★ Enclosure Design Files						
Manufacturing				★ Manufactured Enclosures		★ Manufactured Circuit Boards		
Testing					★ Test Cases			

Figure 4-3: Partial project map example

team. The enclosure development team in turn uses the power control SW deliverable to generate its enclosure design files deliverable that is handed to the manufacturing team. The manufacturing team uses the enclosure design files deliverable to generate its next deliverable, the manufactured enclosures, which are then delivered to the software development team who use the deliverable to generate its SW verify report. This mapping of deliverables shows the critical interdependency between the software, enclosure, and manufacturing teams on the project. The project map can serve as a communication tool to illustrate the interconnectedness of work and to facilitate communication among team members regarding the deliverables and associated activities performed by the global team members.

The global team leader should lead his or her team through the creation of the project map early in the planning phase, and then utilize it throughout the remainder of the project or program lifecycle to drive collaboration, synchronization, and integration of work output across the team.

Communicating Effectively

Communication is defined as one's ability to transmit ideas, receive information, and interact with the environment around you.[9] It is a vital element of any well-managed project or program and is fundamental in establishing goals and objectives, creating networks of individuals and teams, and determining how best to accomplish product and service deliverables.

As the voice of the project, the team leader must be an effective communicator to ensure that all pertinent stakeholders have the right information at the right time to work at their highest levels of productivity. Communicating effectively means ensuring that project messages are delivered clearly, credibly, and concisely. Both senders and receivers of information should have a shared understanding of the messages and contexts of the messages being conveyed. This implies, explicitly, the need for dialogue rather than mere transactional communication to foster effective team performance.

As an extreme example of the importance of good cross-project or program communication, nine months after being launched in 1998, the Mars Climate Orbiter was lost during its first pass around the red planet. The spacecraft became the victim of poor communication between project teams on the Orbiter program. One project team programmed navigational data to be sent to the Orbiter in imperial units (feet, inches, pounds), while another team programmed the Orbiter to receive and interpret the data in Metric units (meters, centimeters, kilograms). The miscommunication, similar to mistakes associated with project Airbus 380 discussed earlier in the chapter, resulted in significant detriment to the program goals. In this case, the Orbiter entered the Martian atmosphere at 57km instead of the intended 140 – 150km, and the $125 million spacecraft was destroyed by heat caused by atmospheric friction. Among the primary contributing factors for the loss were the following, which speak to the importance of good cross-project communication:[10]

- The operational navigation team was not fully informed of the details of the way that the Mars Climate Orbiter was pointed in space;

- The systems engineering function within the program that is supposed to track and double-check all interconnected aspects of the mission was not robust enough;

- Some communications channels among project engineering groups were too informal; and

- The mission navigation team was oversubscribed and its work did not receive peer review.

The three primary elements of effective team communication are listening, reporting, and facilitating. One of the most overlooked aspects of effective communication is active listening. In order for the project or program team leader to learn and understand what is really happening on a project, he or she must spend considerable time listening to the team. As well, in order to fully understand the needs and concerns of the client, the team leader must listen intently and continuously.

Many times, it is the role of the project or program team leader to be the facilitator of communication between members on the team. This first involves setting up effective cross-team communication forums where specific aspects of the project or program can be discussed – such as schedule management, change management, progress reporting, and so on. Along with the forums, the team leader owns setting expectations and establishing cross-team communication guidelines, agendas, and pertinent measures and metrics to be reported and used within each of the forums. During each of the communication forums, the team leader should be prepared to facilitate the communication between the team members, or between various stakeholders, as the case may be.

In global teams, the majority of communication occurs through the use of technology, which can cause a number of challenges due to time delays, poor telephonic connections, background noise, and multiple conversations occurring at one time. On top of that, time zone, cultural, and language differences also have the potential to disrupt effective communication.

These factors require the global team leader to communicate more purposefully, intentionally, formally, and regularly. This includes speaking clearly and precisely, controlling the pace of conversation in meetings so that all members can follow along, listening attentively, reiterating and summarizing key points and decisions, adapting to cultural variables, and using written communication when clarification is needed and to document all decisions and directives.

As pointed out in Chapter Two, informal meetings, which take place in hallways, cafeterias, and other venues where people cross paths in the workplace, are a common occurrence for co-located teams.[11] Global teams do not have the ability to engage in informal meetings between members that are physically distributed, and therefore, must find a way to compensate for this communication channel loss. Focus meetings spawned by conversations that arise in the larger forums should be set up in addition to the larger team meetings. As time progresses on a project or program, the team leader should encourage team members to establish the focus meetings without his or her assistance when the need occurs.

When leading a global team, the project or program leader must be willing to invest time in establishing face-to-face contact with his or her team members. This will most likely require that the team leader be willing to travel to the various sites where team members are located, and do so on a consistent and periodic basis. When cultural and language differences are involved, face-to-face meetings are highly beneficial for both team leader and team members to establish effective communication with one another.

Managing Team Conflict

It is impossible to maintain a conflict-free team environment, as conflict is a way of life when people work together. Conflicts typically emerge because people do not see everything the same way. Each member on a team will demonstrate personal preference, personality traits, ideas, and opinions that occasionally lead to conflict among team members. The conflicts can have either positive or negative effects on individuals, the team collectively, the project, or performance of the business as a whole.

The differences in individual's points of view, when managed properly, can be a source of power for teams because it represents a broader perspective and more possibilities for creative solutions. The positive effects of constructive team conflict include identification of alternatives not yet considered, better solutions to problems, and broader buy-in across the team than if differences aren't discussed.

Of course, team conflict often has negative effects as well. The inability to effectively manage agreement or work through conflict is a major source of team dysfunction. Causes of negative team conflict vary greatly depending upon the situation and individuals involved; however, two of the most common causes are competing interests between team members and communication breakdowns. When this occurs, negative team conflicts can result in reduced productivity, missed delivery dates, hoarding or not sharing vital project information, finger-pointing and scapegoating, reduced collaboration, low team morale, or high team member turnover.

Managing conflict in a global environment can be a more difficult challenge for the team leader. In a global team, conflict can occur quickly due to the high potential for miscommunication, can go unnoticed for a longer period of time because most communication is performed electronically and asynchronously, and can be harder to correct due to a lack of direct face-to-face interaction, personal relationships, and trust. As one project manager told us, "Problems resulting from a simple language miscommunication can take on a life of their own. A simple email exchange can end up frazzling nerves because of a simple cultural misunderstanding."

The global team leader must be hyper-vigilant in identifying conflict between team members, because conflict cannot be resolved if it is not identified. Most times, the global team leader is in the best position to notice conflict in email exchanges between team members, or detect negative conflict during team discussions and meetings. As one global team member explained, "A lot of leaders ignore conflicts between team members, hoping that they will just go away. But they seldom do; they usually just get worse."

So, it is not enough for the global team leader to merely be good at spotting conflict on the team, he or she must also be quick to respond so it is less likely to spiral out of control. Being quick to respond, however, does not mean jumping in whenever a debate of viewpoints is occurring on a team. The global team leader must learn to get involved within certain boundary conditions, such as the following:

- When conflict affects the performance of other team members;

- When conflict jeopardizes achievement of team goals;

- When conflict interferes with team communication;

- When conflict overflows to external stakeholders or partners; and

- When conflict involves a repetitive pattern.

Outside of these boundary conditions, the team leader should allow debate between team members to continue if the debate is moving toward a positive outcome. Doing so will help build team cooperation, collaboration, and cohesiveness.

It is also important for a global team leader to become skilled in determining conflict type once a conflict is identified. Conflict type will determine the general course of action that the team leader will want to follow. Three general types of conflict exist:[12]

- **Task conflict** is an awareness of differences in viewpoints and opinions pertaining to what the team is tasked to do. This type of conflict can be beneficial, and varying viewpoints should be encouraged by the team leader. Task conflict can improve decision quality and ensure that the team is working on the most important set of tasks. The global team leader must act as the facilitator by embracing debate, but also steer the outcome toward achievement of the intended business results.

- **Process conflict** involves debates regarding how the tasks are performed on the team, or how resources are delegated to the tasks. In general, process conflict can be beneficial in improving the effectiveness and efficiency of the team's work, but continued debate can easily turn process conflict into relationship conflict. The global team leader must be vigilant in hearing all viewpoints concerning process, but then be decisive in determining the course of action and set expectation that the process will be followed.

- **Relationship conflict** is an awareness of interpersonal differences. This may include personal differences or hostility and annoyance between team members. Since relationship conflict has a negative effect on individual and team performance, the global team leader must be quick to identify root cause of the conflict and take measures to begin resolving it.

With all types of conflict, the project or program team leader should allow individuals the opportunity to express their differences and allow the team members to establish resolution as the first approach. This requires the establishment of an open team environment, an understanding of the team guidelines for conflict resolution, and may also require coaching on the part of the global team leader. If the individuals in conflict are not successful in finding a solution amongst them, the team leader will need to intervene.

Conflict management presents one more argument for taking the opportunity to establish face-to-face contact between members of a global team. Evidence shows that on virtually-distributed teams, interpersonal bonds are lower, team cohesiveness is lower, members are less satisfied with cross-team interaction, and in general people like each other less than compared to co-located teams.[13] These are all factors created by a lack of trust between members of the team and lead to a higher incidence of negative team conflict. In order to trust one another, people must know one another. The surest way to help the globally-distributed team get to know one another is to get them together physically and allow personal relationships to form.

Making Tough Decisions

Though they vary in complexity, all product and service development projects and programs consist of two core activities – completing tasks and making decisions. Therefore, one can see that effective decision-making is a critical element to team leadership.

There can be thousands of decisions, large and small, that a team leader will encounter during the course of a project or program. To prevent even a small number of these decisions from being barriers to progress, a team leader needs to be proficient in collecting all necessary facts, analyzing the pertinent data, and then driving to a decision. Nothing can be more frustrating and paralyzing to a project or program team than waiting for a decision that prevents forward progress.[14]

The ability of the team leader to make timely decisions will be considerably influenced by their degree of experience, knowledge acquired, and their ability to think of the project from a holistic perspective. By a holistic perspective, we mean that project or program decisions need to be aligned with the goals of the project and the strategic objectives of the business. Losing sight of the strategic reasons for a project while making a series of large and small decisions is a primary reason why some projects become misaligned with the strategic objectives of the business and ultimately fail.

Due to the complexity of most projects and programs, team members need to draw upon a wide array of information to make effective decisions. This means all disciplines and functional teams must be involved in generating information for and participate in the decision-making process.[15] It is no longer the case where engineering utilizes technology-only data, or marketing utilizes customer-only data, or finance utilizes accounting-only data to drive project related decisions.

When the project or program team is distributed across the globe, access to the required information is a greater challenge. Ensuring all required team members and stakeholders participate in the decision-making process presents an additional challenge in the global team environment. Because of these factors, it is important that the global team leader delegates decision rights to the appropriate team members to enable decisions to be made at the local level whenever possible. This increases the probability that the right team members and stakeholders are involved in the decision, and that the required data and information is available.

Delegation of team decisions, however, increases the risk that the decision outcomes can become misaligned to the goals of the project or program. As a safeguard, the team leader must establish boundary conditions that serve as guard rails to prevent goal misalignment. The more concisely and clearly the boundary conditions for a decision are stated, the greater the likelihood that the decision will be effective in accomplishing the direction that is needed and ensuring that the direction is consistent with the business goals driving the need for the project or program.

A wonderful example of a best practice for establishing team decision boundaries based upon business goals is the use of a tool known as the program strike zone.[16] The program strike zone (see Figure 4-4) is an important communication and decision support tool that helps to keep project or program decisions in alignment with the business goals that are driving the need for the development effort.

Program Strike Zone			
Critical Success Factors	**Strike Zone**		**Status**
	Target	Threshold	
Value Proposition ♦ Increase market share in product segment ♦ MSS growth within 6 months of launch ♦ MMS growth one year post launch	 7% 10%	 2% 5%	Green
Schedule ♦ Program plan approval ♦ Initial system 'power on' ♦ Final testing begins ♦ Go-live launch	June 15, 2012 October 1, 2012 March 1, 2013 June 30, 2013	June 30, 2012 November 1, 2012 April 7, 2013 August 15, 2013	Green
Resoures ♦ Team staffing commitments complete ♦ Staffing gaps	June 30, 2012 Project teams staffed at min level	July 15, 2012 No critical path resource gaps	Yellow
Technology ♦ Technology identification complete ♦ Core technology development complete	April 30, 2012 Priority 1,2 tech's delivered	May 15, 2012 Priority 1 tech's delivered	Green
Financials ♦ Program budget ♦ Product cost ♦ Profitability index	100% of plan $8500 2.0	105% of plan $8900 1.8	Red

Figure 4-4: Example program strike zone

The elements of the program strike zone include the business success factors for the project or program, target and control (threshold) limits, and a high level status indicator. In general, a green status indicator signals the global project or program is operating toward achievement of the specific business objectives, a yellow status indicates a heads-up to senior management of a potential problem, and red signals that senior management intervention is needed to proceed.

The success criteria thresholds are the decision boundaries within which the global team must remain within. As long as a decision will not cause the global project or program to move outside of any of the success criteria threshold limits, the team leader and members are empowered to make that decision. If, on the other hand, a decision will cause the project or program to move outside of any success criterion (for example, product cost), the decision must be elevated to the senior management sponsor.

In practice, not all decisions can be delegated to the local level. Whenever a decision outcome will affect more than one sub-team on a project, affect others outside of the project team, or affect the goals of the project, the decision must be made at the core team level, with the global team leader as the decision-maker. In these cases, the team leader must ensure that he or she has the appropriate level of participation to achieve a high-quality decision output.

Providing Recognition and Rewards

Providing recognition and rewards on a project or program can be risky business, even more so for a globally-distributed team. The intent should always be to increase the visibility of the good work being accomplished by the team through recognition and to motivate team members to do their best by means of a reward system.[17] However, care has to be taken not to create a reverse effect where members of the team become de-motivated and trust becomes compromised.

The project or program team leader should ensure that the accomplishments of the team are consistently recognized via communication to the sponsor and other key stakeholders. He or she can extend the recognition to the broader organization as well by tapping into the organization's communications or public relations groups. The primary outcome that the project team leader should look to accomplish through recognition is to increase public awareness of the team's work and to create a sense of team identity on the part of the team members.

Rewards are a bit trickier than recognition because they are usually individually-based, and are many times deemed more valuable due to the fact that they tend to be more tangible in nature. Additionally, rewards are more difficult to provide since the team leader cannot offer pay raises, bonuses, or vacations since team members do not normally report directly to him or her.

This requires the global team leader to be more cautious and creative in providing rewards. Some suggestions for providing rewards include the following:

- Set up a system for project stakeholders and other team members to make recommendations for individual rewards;

- Tap into the broader organizational reward system;

- Provide smaller rewards such as gift certificates or event tickets;

- Provide letters of commendation to the team member's manager; and

- Ensure all members involved in an accomplishment are appropriately rewarded.

To effectively provide recognition and rewards, the global team leader must take stock in the things that they have direct control over and employ them consciously, cautiously, and consistently. Look to recognize and reward team accomplishments over individual accomplishments.

Looking Ahead

In this chapter we looked at what it takes to build and lead a winning global project or program team, and how it differs from building a domestic team. In nearly all cases, a global project or program team is a virtual entity. Therefore the challenge for leaders of global project teams is to create a high performing team that acts as a cohesive unit, while separated by time, distance and culture. We showed how the fundamental elements of team leadership are still valid for a global team, but also how the fundamentals have to be modified and built upon to effectively lead a highly-distributed team in the global environment.

In the next chapter we build upon the knowledge gained in overcoming global execution barriers and challenges by looking at the critical organizational elements that leading global companies have established to create sustainable and improving global execution practices.

CHAPTER FIVE

Achieving Sustainable Global Team Success

"Anyone can hold the helm when the sea is calm"
- Publilius Syrus, Latin writer of maxims

Scott Jones, who was introduced in Chapter One, was feeling the pressures of globalization. As Director of New Product Development, Jones realized that as his company began the process of growing globally they were moving away from a comfortable position within a niche market segment of their industry, to a position that would make them a direct competitor to the industry leaders – all of which are *global* leaders.

When Jones utilized his network of cross-industry experts to understand what it means to be a leading global company, he was able to summarize his learnings in three key points:

- Global leaders are able to execute their product and service development projects and program in a globally-distributed environment as effectively as their toughest competitors do in a domestic environment;

• Global leaders consistently achieve their strategic goals as a result of a tight alignment between strategy and execution output; and

• Global leaders use global execution as a competitive advantage to put distance between themselves and their competitors.

Jones learned that global execution leadership means more than achieving repeatable success in developing new products and services in a global team environment. It means establishing continual improvement in their new product or service development process – continually raising the bar on global team execution performance – and business results.

Chapters Three and Four presented leadership best practices for overcoming the barriers and challenges that a company will encounter in their quest to achieve repeatable global execution success. This chapter builds upon these best practices, and explores the critical factors that leading global companies have used to achieve sustainable competitive advantage through global product and service development.

Using Technology Effectively

Mona Harmond, a global program manager for a well-known consumer products company, describes what used to be a common sight in her company's globally-distributed offices. "Picture a group of people sitting at a table, surrounding a speakerphone in the middle, trying to conduct a team meeting with three other groups of people in three different geographical locations. If it was a well-run meeting, a common PowerPoint presentation would be projected in each of the three conference rooms and used to direct the conversation of the team."

Even though this was a common sight, Harmond agrees that it was not a form of optimal team communication and collaboration. "Even though people were communicating verbally instead of relying on email, this form of communication still presented some challenges," explained Harmond. Among the challenges: the largest group of people typically dominated the conversation; many side discussions would take place while other locations were talking; the more introverted team members would fail to participate in the discussion; and the collective team often failed to fully understand the meeting outcomes, next steps to be taken and by whom, and key decisions that had been made.

"What we learned from these early experiences," explains Harmond, "was that technology, if not selected and used properly, will result in teams reverting to tried and true technologies even though they are not the most optimum solution." Harmond's learning is consistent with virtual team studies which show that the vast majority of global teams rely on e-mail, telephone calls, and face-to-face meetings to do their work.[1] It is important to note that technology will not solve communication problems, but rather it can serve to improve it.

The Role of Technology

The primary role of technology in global teamwork is one of overcoming the challenges created by time and distance.[2] Successful use of technology on a global team hinges upon understanding how the team will communicate and collaborate, understanding how technology can be leveraged to improve team communication and collaboration, matching technology selection to communication and collaboration methods and practices, and then using the technology efficiently to improve the team's performance.

Many times large investments in communication and collaboration technologies have failed to pay for themselves because the technology was initially selected based on false financial estimates of productivity gains or because of pressures to implement technology solutions used by industry leaders, rather than selecting solutions to integrate into the team culture and need. In nearly all successful examples of technologically-enhanced team communication and collaboration, the technology was selected and used based on how well it enhanced established methods and processes.[3]

Technology Selection

The senior leaders of an organization, in collaboration with global team leaders, should select electronic technologies that best meet the needs and usage of the global teams and that integrate with the current suite of tools used within the organization. Always use technology tools that complement the culture and that are appropriately selected based on need. Technology should always increase team productivity and should be evaluated based upon that measure.

It should be pointed out that there is no ideal set of technologies for all teams. There are basic technologies that most all teams will benefit from – such as the telephone, e-mail, and calendaring and scheduling systems – but since all organizations are unique, so are their virtual communication and collaboration needs. The senior leaders and global team leaders must therefore develop a clear strategy for matching technology options to the communication and collaboration needs of their global teams.

The technology selection strategy should consider four primary factors:

- Team interactions;
- Communication and collaboration methods;
- Contextual differences; and
- Team tasks.

Team interactions. There are three primary ways in which members of a global project or program team interact: through conversations, through transactions, and through collaborations.

Conversational interaction is a free exchange of information between team members for the primary purpose of knowledge exchange, discovery, or relationship building. Conversational interaction is free of constraints and does not use a central repository of information.

Transactional interactions occur when a team member exchanges something tangible (e.g. requirements document, project plan, design file) with one or more members of his or her team. The transaction is usually constrained by a need and expectation (stated or implied) by the receiver for the deliverable.

Collaborative interaction occurs when two or more members of a team work together to complete a task, solve a problem, brainstorm new ideas, or develop a common deliverable. Collaborative interaction requires a common electronic workspace and a repository to store completed and in-process work.

Communication and collaboration methods. Once a global project or program team understands the types of interaction they will be engaged in, the next step is to understand which method of communication and collaboration best meets their needs – synchronous, asynchronous, or a combination of both.

Synchronized communication is direct communication between team members where the communications are time synchronized.[4] This means all members are present and communicating at the same time, but may be separated by time zones. Synchronous communication and collaboration methods are best for interactive activities such as brainstorming, problem solving, decision-making, and team status reporting.

Asynchronous communication occurs when the team members involved in the communication are not present at the same time. Therefore time delays occur between communication exchanges between team members. Asynchronous communication and collaboration methods work well for information and data exchange that does not have to be completed in real time.

Contextual differences. One of the most distinguishing features of a global team is context. Team context involves the way in which team members live and work relative to a specific geographical area. A global team must learn to work within multiple contexts and the technologies they select must take into account the constraints that the geographical contexts create. The primary contextual factors include physical infrastructure, culture and language, time zone boundaries, and team size.

Physical infrastructure involves the capability and availability of the basic utilities such as electrical power, telephone, and internet upon which all communication and collaboration technologies rely. Differences in availability, reliability, and maturity of the physical infrastructure will impact the various choices in communication and collaboration technologies from which one can choose.

Culture and language may affect the use of various communication and collaboration technologies because differences in cultural norms and languages lead to different media preferences and comfort levels on the part of the people using the technologies. For example, asynchronous communication technologies such as email may be preferred by team members who are not proficient in speaking English, or who are not comfortable resolving team disagreements or conflicts using synchronous technologies such as video conferencing because doing so compromises deep-rooted cultural norms.

Time zone boundaries create a unique set of challenges for the use of various technologies. Multiple time zone separation between global team members may require some members to work much earlier or later than their standard working hours. In such cases, the utility of some synchronous technologies (such as video conferencing) diminishes as people are less responsive to coming into the office during off hours to attend a meeting or to collaborate with their team members in other parts of the world. Work-life balance issues could cause them to prefer to use telephone or e-mail technologies as an alternative.

Team size must also be taken into account when developing the technology selection strategy as some large collaboration technologies may be too complicated for small teams and some simple communication technologies may be insufficient for large teams. For example, office teleconferencing systems are usually limited to three participants. As well, large teams can also make some audio conferencing systems such as bridge networks ineffective because of difficulties in keeping conversations focused and team members fully engaged.

Team tasks. The final factor in developing a technology selection strategy involves looking at the relationship between the types of tasks undertaken by the global team and the technologies they use to help them complete those tasks. We generalize team tasks into two primary categories: low-complexity tasks and high-complexity tasks.

Low-complexity tasks are those that involve low interdependence and require limited collaboration between team members. Most conversational and transactional interactions fall into this category. For these types of tasks, asynchronous technologies such as email, blogs, data repositories, and websites are completely sufficient.

High-complexity tasks are those that involve a high degree of collaboration and information sharing between team members in order to complete the task. Team members are highly interdependent when working high-complexity tasks and the technologies they use must support the synchronous collaboration of workflow. For these tasks, technologies such as videoconferencing, whiteboards, common workspaces, and shared data repositories are beneficial.

Creating a Technology Strategy

By analyzing the various factors involved in a global team's communication and collaboration practices, the senior leaders and global team leaders can develop a technology strategy for the organization.

The analysis does not have to be a complicated undertaking. A simple mapping of the various communication and collaboration factors that will be in play for a firm's global teams to the various technology options may be sufficient to formulate a strategy. Figure 5-1 illustrates an example of a mapping outcome.

Factors	Communication Technologies				Collaboration Technologies			
	Email	Blogs	Telephone	Others	Website	Shared Workspace	Data Repository	Others
Team Interaction								
Conversational	+		+					
Transactional								
Collaborative						+		
Communication and Collaboration Methods								
Synchronous			+			+		
Asynchronous	+						+	
Team Contexts								
Physical Infrastructure			-					-
Culture and Language			-					
Time Zones	+		-			+	+	+
Team Size	-			+				
Task Types								
Low Complexity								
High Complexity	-					+		+

Figure 5-1: An example of communication and collaboration technology mapping

As the example demonstrates, the technology mapping shows the primary communication and collaboration factors that must be considered along with the various technologies options under consideration. It should be pointed out that each organization will have its own unique set of communication and collaboration factors and candidate technologies.

A simple +/- evaluation of whether a particular technology option either supports (+) or hampers (-) the communication and collaboration factors specific to the organization will provide sufficient information to develop a firm's technology strategy for its global teams.

By way of example, the information contained in Figure 5-1 represents the technology mapping results performed by Scott Jones in conjunction with Keytron's Chief Information Officer and their global team leaders. Based upon the mapping, the technology strategy for the firm included the following:

- The global teams are engaged in both conventional and collaborative transactions that are performed both asynchronously and synchronously; therefore, email and telephone conversation, along with a shared workspace and a data repository are necessary to meet this firm's needs.

- Physical infrastructure limitations in one or more geographies will likely prevent the use of more sophisticated technologies such as video conferencing and product lifecycle management (PLM) systems.

- A large team size and highly-collaborative (high-complexity) workflow put constraints on the use of email communication and points to the need for audio conferencing capabilities that will support a large number of team members.

Two additional factors must be considered in the development of a firm's technology strategy: technology maturity and technology overload. Global organizations are often quick to adopt new technologies in hopes that they will help them to improve their communication and collaboration practices; however, new technology often brings both a user learning curve and technological bugs that in truth may significantly hamper a team's communication and collaboration effectiveness instead of improve it. When this happens, we find that the teams eventually revert back to tried-and-true technologies, leaving the organization with a significantly low return-on-technology-investment ratio.

Information technology (IT) organizations within many firms bring in a plethora of tools to help with team communication and collaboration. After all, this is the traditional mission of most IT organizations. The problem with this approach is that most times global teams end up with more technology options than they need, or that are useful. This problem points to a misalignment of goals between global product and service development organizations and the IT organization. To prevent technology overload, the goals of a firm's IT organization must align to the needs of the product and service development teams so that technology selection is indeed driven by global team usage and need.

Investing in Relationships and Trust

Raphael Sangura is an educator and industry consultant who works with companies that have moved to a globally-distributed product or service development model. He has consistently observed something interesting within the companies that he works with. "When I discuss the importance of face-to-face contact between members of globally-distributed teams, I get unanimous agreement from senior managers, middle managers, project or program team leaders, and team members that getting the product or service development team together on multiple occurrences is critical to developing personal relationships and trust," explains Sanguara. However, when the global project or program managers from these firms attempt to get funding and time to bring the teams together for face-to-face meetings, their requests are often denied by either the middle managers or the senior managers. When asked about this predicament, Sanguara concluded that, "Either middle and senior managers don't buy in to the importance of the face-to-face meetings, or they don't fully understand the return they will gain from their investment in money and time."

The benefit versus cost of bringing a globally-distributed team together is often debated within businesses. However, leading global companies no longer debate this issue. For them, the act of bringing their globally-distributed teams together on a periodic basis is embedded in their project or program planning and execution practices.

There should be no debate within your organization either. The benefits of team face-to-face meetings are well documented in case studies, industry research, and team member testimonials. The short list of benefits that are consistently cited include accelerated establishment of relationships, increased personal bonds and trust between team members, a clearer understanding of roles and responsibilities, an increased commitment and accountability for meeting team deliverables and deadlines, broader cross-cultural awareness, and establishment of direct lines of communication between team members. When realized, these benefits move the group of individuals assigned to a global project or program to a higher dgree of team performance.

These benefits are realized in large part because of an increase in social presence on a team. Social presence is the degree to which personal connection is established between team members. The higher the level of social presence, the stronger the personal connection between team members. Relationships, personal bonds, trust, commitment, and communication all depend upon strong personal connection. Face-to-face meetings have the highest degree of social presence than any of the collaboration tools and medium used by globally-distributed teams (see Figure 5-2).

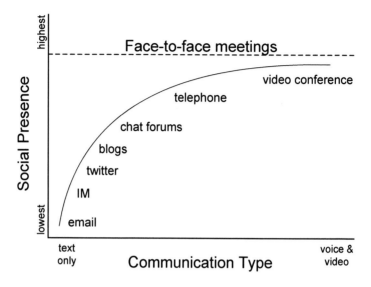

Figure 5-2: Degree of social presence of communication types

As explained in Chapter Four, trust within a global team is at the core of effective collaboration between the team members. Trust, however, is built upon personal relationships. Therefore trust cannot be established on a team if its team members do not know one another. By bringing members of a global team together at the beginning of a project or program, relationships begin to form between team members, and personal bonds begin to strengthen. This is due to the fact that team members begin to know one another as people with personal lives, varying personalities, families, and common interests outside of work. It becomes easier to trust one another when this level of understanding about one another and personal bonds are allowed to form.

Team meetings, especially those held early in the product or service development effort, must be expertly facilitated to conduct meaningful activities that foster social presence intentionally aimed to build relationships not only on a professional level, but also on a personal level.

With relationships and trust beginning to be established, an increased commitment to the people on the team and to the team goals begins to form. As one global team member told us, "My deadlines now no longer affect a voice on the phone or a person writing an email – they now affect my friends and colleagues. I feel that my tasks are much more important to complete because I don't want to let down people I know." The implication of this is important for globally-distributed teams. By creating bonds between people through a face-to-face meeting, commitment and productivity increases at a rapid pace.

Global leaders and other best practice companies use the face-to-face meetings to increase collaboration between team members as well as other stakeholders involved with the team by centering the face-to-face gatherings on work events. It is a good idea to hold an initial face-to-face meeting early in the lifecycle of the project, generally in the initiation or planning phase. Two important items that can be worked on collaboratively as a team in the initial face-to-face meeting are the creation of the team charter and completion of the project or program map (see Chapter Four).

Creating the team charter as a team helps the members to agree on the common end-state and goals that the project or program is trying to achieve. Additionally, it serves to clarify the roles and responsibilities of each member of the global team, identify all primary and secondary stakeholders, and raise visibility of critical milestones and timeline events. The charter is also a tool that can be used to capture the team's guiding principles that will be followed throughout the project or program. These principles can serve as the basis for creating team norms and expectations.

By creating the project or program map collaboratively as a team, the interdependencies between the team members become apparent through the identification of cross-team deliverables. In the process of mapping deliverables to those dependent upon them, commitment between team members becomes ingrained partly because relationships, roles, and responsibilities are being understood. With guiding principles determined and relationships established in the face-to-face meeting, meeting deliverable content and dates now become personal commitments with team members accountable to one another.

By getting the globally-distributed team together in a face-to-face meeting, the global team leader now has an opportunity to begin increasing the cultural awareness within the team. One should not lose the opportunity to conduct at least one team building activity where members can share important aspects of their national culture with all members of the team. This will increase team member's knowledge of one another, of the various cultures represented on the team, certain nuances associated with the cultures, and particular cultural sensitivities to take in to account when interacting with other team members. Additional information on cultural awareness is presented later in this chapter.

Since personal ties degrade over time, leading global companies have learned that periodic face-to-face meetings are required to maintain a high level of global team performance and commitment to the project or program goals. This is an important concept to understand. Investing in an initial face-to-face meeting is good, but not nearly sufficient for success. Face-to-face meetings are necessary throughout the project or program, especially when conflicts arise, new members come on board, and project or program goals shift. All of these occurrences can begin to erode the personal bonds that are established in the initial face-to-face meeting.

The list of benefits of face-to-face meetings is long and powerful. At the core of the benefits are the foundational elements for establishment of a high performance team – relationships, trust, commitment, accountability, clear roles and responsibilities, and direct communication. The value is clear:

if an enterprise wants to increase the performance and output of its globally-distributed teams, it must plan for and invest in periodic face-to-face meetings. This means that senior managers must provide the funding and time for face-to-face meetings, while global team leaders must include face-to-face gatherings as part of their process and be capable of effectively facilitating the meetings.

Modifying the Team Delivery System

Time can be the primary enemy of the global project or program team leader. Difficulties coordinating work and driving effective communication across multiple time zones is well known and documented. So too are tools and techniques to help resolve these difficulties.

In addition to time zone challenges, time also presents a more perplexing and potentially dangerous challenge for the global team leader. In this case, we are referring to the length of time that can lapse between project milestones or team deliverables. Globally-distributed projects or programs will face a loss of time efficiency due to their complexity. Time zone challenges hit you immediately and even the newest of global team leaders learns quickly how to cope with his or her particular challenges, but time lapse challenges unfortunately do not confront you as rapidly and as obviously. Many times they do not become evident until a project moves outside its success control limits or until it even fails outright.

Failure analysis often shows that the greater the amount of time between project or program milestones, or between team member deliverables, the greater the risk that a project or program will go off track or fail. The probability of failure increases as does the severity of impact as time increases between milestones or deliverables as illustrated in Figure 5-3.

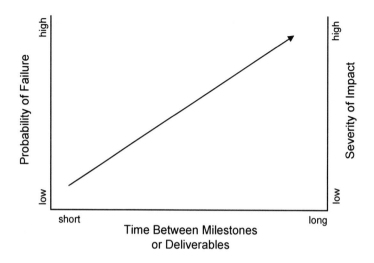

Figure 5-3: Increasing risk with increasing time between milestones and deliverables

Distributed team members have to perform much of their work and create their deliverables based upon a series of assumptions. When incorrect assumptions occur, they are discovered and corrected once work is completed or through direct communication and collaboration with other team members. With a decrease in direct communication, lack of informal meetings, and limited synchronous collaboration between distributed team members as compared to co-located teams, it is rare that incorrect assumptions are discovered through communication and collaboration. Rather, they are usually found when work and deliverables are created and inconsistencies between what was delivered and what was expected are discovered through the integration process.

When a large amount of time passes between deliverable creation and hand-off, the likelihood that multiple incorrect assumptions have been made will increase. This normally results in work that has to be corrected once the incorrect assumptions are discovered. This is commonly referred to as rework. Any time rework occurs, productivity decreases, time is lost, additional money has to be invested, and the project or program goals are compromised.

To combat this negative factor of time, teams that execute most effectively in a global environment adopt what we refer to as a *rapid delivery model*. In a rapid delivery model, work output is decomposed into small deliverables which can be worked on and completed within a short period of time. With a rapid delivery model, assumptions can then be tested in an accelerated manner and any rework required will be relatively minor. This small, step-by-incremental-step model is highly effective and rather standard on successful global team endeavors.

The intentionally designed and scheduled rapid delivery model works because it forces team members to communicate and collaborate on a continuous basis throughout the lifecycle of the project or program. When this model is utilized, the need to create a project or program map increases, as this tool becomes the team's focal point for planning and managing rapid development of its deliverables.

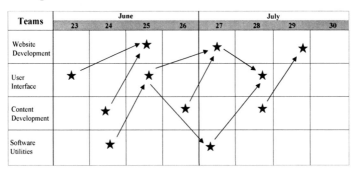

Figure 5-4: Example rapid delivery program map

Figure 5-4 illustrates an example of a program map created by a globally-distributed team which utilized the rapid delivery model to complete its work. As shown in the figure, each team has a series of deliverables that are separated by two or three weeks in duration. With constant focus on rapid development and hand-off of deliverables between teams it becomes difficult for the work of a global program to veer too far off course before the problem is discovered and corrected.

Creating a Learning and Maturing Organization

It is important to realize that today's leading global product and service companies did not start out in a leadership position. In most cases, becoming highly proficient in developing their products and services in a globally-distributed model took years to achieve, with both successes and failures along the way.

What *is* significant about these companies however is that they continued to learn from both their successes and failures, and improved their processes, methods, tools, and practices from one product or service generation to the next. By doing so, they continued to transform their companies from local organizations to global organizations. This is what it means to be a learning and maturing organization.

Taking Time to Learn

In order to learn from one's successes and failures, you must first pause to reflect on why you succeeded or failed. Surprisingly, many organizations never take the time to evaluate what they are doing, why it is working or not, and what needs to change in order to move closer to their globalization goals. They just keep plowing forward hoping that the inertia pushing them forward is in the *right* direction.

This may be good in the small number of cases where an enterprise remains on track and their global environment does not experience significant change. However, for the large majority of cases, failing to stop, reflect, and adjust serves to move an organization further from their globalization goals, not closer.

One of the best practices for periodically evaluating a firm's progress toward meeting its globalization goals is the use of a retrospective process. Retrospectives are a series of events where team members who have a perspective to share meet at critical points during the project or program lifecycle to discuss what is working and what needs to be improved. The intent is to capture key lessons while a project or program is in flight, and apply improvements during the remainder of the lifecycle.[5]

Retrospectives differ from the more traditional post-project audit or traditional lessons learned activities. In many companies, a post-project audit meeting is held following the conclusion or cancellation of a project and is typically led by the project or program manager. Because this meeting occurs at the end of the development cycle it is too late to implement corrections on the project or program that is currently in flight. At best, learnings can be applied to the next project or program. In our experience, the post-project audit is many times held as an after thought without a defined, objective process and does not lead to actionable change to project or program team practices.

The short list of advantages of using the retrospective methodology includes the following:

- Many times teams focus only on the negative aspects of their performance and forget the positive. Retrospectives also explore what is working well on a project or program, and ensures the practices are reinforced and repeated.

- Retrospectives allow an organization to make positive changes to projects or programs that are currently in-flight, therefore they don't have to wait twelve months or more to realize the benefits of their learnings.

- Teams learn best when they solve immediate problems. As part of the retrospective method, teams focus on the few but critical opportunities to improve, and develop specific action plans to drive changes in their practices. Theses action plans are owned by various members of the project or program team who drive them to implementation.

Monika Billings talks about why her company uses a retrospective approach to capture key learnings from their global program teams. "At our company, very few development teams are located in the same state or country, much less in the same building. We have teams spread across approximately 290 locations in 45 countries and have found that post-project audits are ineffective with highly-distributed teams. Retrospectives, on the other hand, are quite effective because of the use of a trained facilitator who is an expert in extracting the key issues and learnings from our diverse and distributed workforce." Importantly, the retrospective is built into the project plan at critical points so as to intentionally take time to learn and improve.

When applied most effectively, a trained, objective facilitator – someone other than the global team leader – guides the team through an analysis of what is working well and what is not, and then helps the program or project team generate ideas for improvement and what they want to do differently. To apply the learnings, the facilitator then works with the team to create actionable plans to improve both effectiveness and efficiency. Learnings are applied and behaviors are changed through the continuous monitoring and tracking of action plan implementation and communication of progress to senior stakeholders within the organization.

Whether an organization uses the retrospective method or another method to capture its organizational learnings is not the most critically-important factor in creating a learning organization. What is important is that the organization consistently invests the time and effort to stop, reflect, learn, and improve continuously over time.

Creating Cross-Cultural Awareness

As a firm begins to expand its product and service development efforts into other geographies, the organization (especially its global project or program teams) becomes a culturally-blended entity. National culture will influence team members' abilities to deal with ambiguous situations, their ability to work and think independently, how they view personal accountability, and how comfortable they are directly interfacing with people at higher levels of the organization. As a result, it becomes necessary to learn about and embrace the cultural norms, beliefs, and behaviors within each country in which the company is involved.

Much has been written about how people from the home country must become sensitive to other cultures represented on a team. But in reality, all members of the team must develop awareness and sensitivity to each culture represented. The most common approach we see for creating cultural awareness and sensitivity is to create courses such as 'working with people from China' or 'working with people from America,' and then require all team members to participate in the course. Others hire consultants to facilitate discussion and develop cultural awareness among members of the organizations. Although these are the most common approaches, they are insufficient if an organization really wants its people to be able to act differently in a culturally-blended environment.

A better approach is to invest in the time and effort to bring people together, allow them to interact with one another, and learn from one another about their cultures. Jennifer Becker, a global program manager, gives an example that demonstrates the difference between taking a cultural awareness course and actually interacting with people within the culture. "The cultural sensitivity course I took on Latin American cultures that was offered by a consulting firm brought in by my company actually cautioned that people in Mexico may break for a siesta in the afternoon. When I met my team members in Guadalajara, they were aware of this caution in the training course, and quickly assured me that they wouldn't be taking any siestas. They were really pretty offended that the course indicated that they might be found napping in the middle of the work day."

Once team members become aware of some of the myths and actual nuances concerning the cultures on the team and associate the behaviors that result from the nuances to actual people, they can then begin to learn about the sensitivities associated with the cultural nuances. Geert Hofstede identified several cultural factors which may lead to team member sensitivities on a global team. These factors are power-distance, uncertainty avoidance, individual-collectivism, and long term-short term orientation.[6]

Power distance refers to the power distribution within an organization and the extent to which the less powerful members of organizations accept that power is distributed unequally. In low power distance cultures (United States, Great Britain, Germany, Switzerland) people relate to one another more as equals regardless of formal positions. Subordinates are more comfortable with and demand the right to contribute to and critique the decision making of those in power. In high power distance countries (Malaysia, Singapore, Brazil, India, China), people accept power relations that are more autocratic and hierarchical. Subordinates acknowledge the power of others simply based on where they are situated in certain formal, hierarchical positions. Decisions made by individuals in highly-placed positions are rarely questioned or critiqued by subordinates.

Differences in power distance acceptance can affect the way in which members of a globally-distributed team are willing to collaborate. Some team members may feel uncomfortable collaborating with people of a higher ranking within the organizational hierarchy or presenting to senior managers. Knowing how team members perceive power distance will help the global project team leader drive appropriate levels of collaboration across the team and with various stakeholders, as well as help him or her spot power distance discomfort if it occurs.

Uncertainty avoidance reflects the extent to which members of a society attempt to cope with uncertainty. Uncertainty avoidance may affect the ways in which team members carry out their tasks autonomously. Team members from high uncertainty-avoidance cultures (Japan, Belgium, France, South Korea, Brazil, Italy) are less likely to be comfortable in roles that are poorly defined or have ambiguous goals. They prefer rules and structured circumstances. By contrast, team members from low uncertainty-avoidance cultures (United States, Great Britain, Hong Kong, Singapore) are quite comfortable in ambiguous situations and are more willing to take higher levels of risk in order to achieve an outcome. The global team leader has to be careful to match task assignments to individuals possessing the appropriate level of uncertainty avoidance.

Individual-collectivism refers to the degree to which team members of a culture prefer to act as individuals rather than as members of a collective group. People from high individualism cultures (United States, Australia, Great Britain, Italy, France, Germany) are comfortable being singled out individually or working alone, as well as working within a team environment. People from high collectivism cultures (most of Asia and Latin America) value a strong identity with the group or team, and tend to put the needs of the group before their own. Implications of individual-collectivism on a globally-distributed team include differences in team members' expectations about team unity, differences in personal bonding, and the ways in which rewards and recognitions should be handled.

Long versus short-term orientation describes a society's "time horizon," or the importance attached to the future versus the past and present. In long term-oriented societies, values include perseverance, thrift, and having a sense of humility. In short term-oriented societies there is an orientation for quick results, personal steadiness and stability, and respect for tradition.

In addition to Hofstede's factors, other cultural factors which have to be acknowledged, understood, and factored in to a global team leader's awareness include gender bias, assertiveness, and language proficiency.

David Myers describes gender as the characteristics, whether biological or socially influenced, by which people define male and female and a gender role as a set of behavior expectations for male and females.[7] Currently, researchers are acknowledging that gender differences have little to no biological basis and are focusing on gender differences as a result of the social, cultural, and environmental influences.[8] So, to a great extent, what individuals and managers are faced with is a wide variety of gender stereotyping that has permeated society globally.

Culturally, this can be an important consideration for the global team leader depending upon the nations and cultures that are represented on their team. This stereotyping may influence some culture's views of women in business, and may cause challenges for the global team leader if cultures that do not value or permit women to actively participate in business roles are represented on the team.

The degree of assertiveness can be seen as an asset or a liability in managing teams depending upon your cultural orientation. Robert J. House, Director of the Global Leadership and Organizational Behavior Effectiveness Research Program at the Wharton School, has spent the past several years studying how different cultures throughout the world define leadership. He and his colleagues have found that definitions and perceptions of leadership vary considerably from culture to culture.

One of their most important findings is that there are culturally-contingent attributes that can help or hinder leadership. What is strength in one culture may be a considerable impediment in another culture. Different cultural groups may vary in their conceptions of the most important characteristics of leadership. In some cultures, one might need to take strong, decisive action in order to be seen as a leader, while in other cultures, consultation and a democratic approach may be the preferred approach to exercising effective leadership. For example, the U.S. individualistic approach of "brutal honesty" and the Japanese collectivistic norm of "face saving" may resonate well with some or turn others off in a cross-cultural team setting.[9] The global team leader must become proficient in managing assertive team members who may limit or prevent the participation of other less assertive members on the team.

Language proficiency is a contributing factor to achieving *shared understanding* within a global team. Shared understanding, in the context of a team relates to the concept of "mental models" of the team. A team's "mental model" refers to an organizational understanding or mental representation of knowledge that is shared by the team members.[10] There are many factors that contribute to the effectiveness of a shared understanding with one being language use and proficiency. Many teams conduct their team communications and meetings in English; however, in practical terms, especially in some widely and culturally-dispersed teams, there may be several languages in use during the life of the project and its activities. It has been commonly stated that the use of multiple languages on global teams is important and appreciated by many of the other team members, even if you don't speak all languages fluently.

No doubt, there is a lack of full participation of those team members not fluent in the primary language used on a team. These language disconnects can cause a loss and mis-interpretation of critical information during meetings and other communications. This is further worsened in globally-distributed team communication by the fact that more is lost in communication due to the lack of visual cues available in face-to-face communication because so much of global team communication occurs virtually. This slows down communication and may drastically impact the level and quality of what is communicated. This, of course, increases the challenge to the global team leader. The team leader must take extra precaution and time to insure that communications, both oral and written, are received and understood. Redundancy and follow-up on communication is a key part of ensuring this success.

An awareness of the cultural factors that are present on the team is good knowledge for the global project or program team leader, but that knowledge is really of no value unless it is put to use toward leading the team more effectively. Effective global team leaders go beyond gaining an awareness of the cultural nuances present on their team and becoming more astute in understanding the sensitivities associated with the nuances. They use that information to modify how they lead the people on the team and how they manage the team communication, collaboration, and decision-making processes.

A tool that is useful for a global team leader to develop his or her cultural leadership strategy is the cultural assessment.[11] Cultural assessments are valuable in evaluating how a new global project or program stands with respect to the cultural factors. But, they can become quite complex and require an inordinate amount of the global team leader's time to generate. We advocate a simple approach which may be less precise, but provides the team leader all the information necessary to develop a cultural strategy for the team. Figure 5-5 is an example of a simple cultural assessment tool that can be easily implemented to help develop a cultural strategy.

Cultural Dimension	Sensitivity Low ◄——————————————► High				
	1	2	3	4	5
Japanese Team					
Power Distance				X	
Uncertainty Avoidance				X	
Individualism		X			
Long-term Orientation				X	
English Proficiency			X		
Assertiveness	X				
American Team					
Power Distance	X				
Uncertainty Avoidance		X			
Individualism					X
Long-term Orientation		X			
English Proficiency					X
Assertiveness			X		
Chinese Team					
Power Distance					X
Uncertainty Avoidance			X		
Individualism					X
Long-term Orientation					X
English Proficiency	X				
Assertiveness				X	

Figure 5-5: Cultural assessment tool

The global team leader can use this tool to assess the sensitivity to each of the cultural factors that may affect his or her team. Obviously, the sensitivities will vary from person to person on the team, so it is best to evaluate the team from a national perspective, not an individual perspective. For example, if the team has representation from Japan, the team leader can assume that these people will score lower on individualism. He or she must then determine just how low on the sensitivity scale the Japanese team members relative to the rest of the team members. Conversely, the American team members will likely score high on individualism. This information can then be used to develop a team unity strategy, task structure, and rewards system for the global team.

The key to using the cultural assessment effectively is to identify the extremes (either very low sensitivity or very high sensitivity) to the cultural factors. When extremes are identified, adjustments must be made in the way a global team leader manages his or her team.

For example, in Figure 5-5 it was determined that the team members from Shanghai had a low proficiency for understanding spoken English. Due to this cultural factor, the team leader cannot rely exclusively on verbal communication, but must repeat any verbal instructions and critical discussions in written form to ensure that the team in Shanghai understands and is engaged in the dialogue, thus receiving acknowledgement via written feedback.

Since everyone is the product of their own cultures, we need to increase both our self awareness and our cross-cultural awareness in order to better understand one another. The global team leader needs to be the champion for cross-cultural leadership and a role model for good culturally-sensitive behavior. Stephanie Quappe and Cantafore Giovanna provide six useful behaviors for a global team leader to demonstrate: [12]

1. Admit that we don't know. Much of our current knowledge regarding other cultures may be incorrect.

2. Suspend judgments. Do not make generalized or stereotypical assumptions about team member's cultures.

3. Show empathy. By listening and caring about others, we learn how other people would like to be treated.

4. Systematically check our assumptions. Ask for feedback and constantly make sure you clearly understand the situation.

5. Become comfortable with ambiguity. Accept the fact that globally-distributed teams will be more

complex and that many things will not be totally clear.

6. Celebrate diversity. Recognize and espouse the value of differing viewpoints, opinions, and ways of doing things.

Failure to make adjustments due to cultural factors will decrease the project or program's probability of success. Adjustments made to the way the global team leader manages the project or program as a result of the cultural factors should be documented in the team charter and agreed to as part of the team norms.

Team Leader Training

The critical skills necessary for successful and sustainable global project or program execution are primarily those of the global team leader. It is the global team leader who integrates the team and keeps it running as a distributed but cohesive unit.

There are very few global team leaders, however, who come to the job with the full suite of skills and competencies needed (see Chapter Six). The organization, and in particular its senior managers must be willing to invest continually in the learning and development of its global team leaders. This is hardly an easy task.

As Scott Jones, whom we have heard from throughout this text, explains, "I would gladly provide the training needed to develop my global program managers. My problem is that I don't know what training they really need and where I can get it." This is one of the biggest problems in global team leader development. Because the skills and competencies needed for effective global team leadership are so broad and diverse, a training and development curriculum specific to the job is lacking.

The most common failing of organizations regarding global team leader training is to rely on widely available project management training and certification programs that exist today. While project management is a critical aspect of leading global teams, it is only one aspect of the global team leader's competency. The answer is to understand fully the core competency model of the global team leader detailed in Chapter Six, and then customize training and development for the organization's team leaders based upon the strengths and gaps as compared to the model.

Although this can be fairly burdensome in the beginning, investment in the initial and continual assessment against the competency model will pay dividends as the global team leaders begin to fill the gaps required to effectively and consistently lead globally-distributed teams. Their competency and effectiveness will continually increase over time, increasing their individual value as a team leader as well as the organization's ability to effectively compete in the global market.

Changing Behavior by Changing Rewards

Most organizations that embark on a global strategy have well-established rewards and recognition systems that favor individual and functional performance, and de-emphasize team-based performance. Leading global companies have learned over time that their reward and recognition systems have to be modified to emphasize and reinforce team performance in order to build a sustainable global execution success record.

All teams, whether local or global, share at least one common attribute: to be highly effective, they require a supportive reward system where personal success is dependent upon team success.[13] Effective execution in a global team environment requires a high degree of collaboration between team members; therefore, the reward system for global teams must put a premium on collaborative success. Performance measures must be designed to include working across geographical boundaries, successful integration across cultures, sharing of information, completing interdependent deliverables, sharing critical information to support virtual teamwork, and meeting team objectives. This requires rewards that are based upon results instead of effort.[14]

The challenge is to create a fit between the characteristics of the individuals on the global team, the characteristics of the organization, and the characteristics of the reward system. Because teams can differ greatly in their mission, structure, processes, and team member make-up and distribution, no one reward system design will be universally effective. Each organization must design its own system. This, unfortunately, is not a simple task. A common approach is to design a reward system that combines both skill-based and performance-based rewards, all of which are heavily influenced by the achievement of project or program objectives.

Skill-based Rewards

Skill-based rewards are used on a global project or program team to motivate the development of functional expertise of the global team leader as well as the global team members. Additionally, skill-based rewards are used to provide focus on the development of cross-functional knowledge and virtual team operating skills that are needed to effectively participate and drive global team collaboration.

Depth of expertise in one or more functional areas utilized on the global team is often critical to global execution success. Skill-based incentives reward individuals for developing deeper levels of expertise within a knowledge area. Additionally, it helps to retain the technical expertise within the organization. Typical implementations of skill-based rewards involve defining multiple levels of expertise within a knowledge area (such as engineering, marketing, manufacturing), and when individuals demonstrate that their competency exceeds their current level, they are then promoted to the next higher level.

Performance-based Rewards

To ensure skill-based rewards are influenced by team results, the individual must be able to prove that he or she has demonstrated that the skills within an expertise level were used to help further team collaboration and contributed to the success of the project or program on which they participated. Team-based application must be a defining criterion for promotion to the next level of expertise. This is the basis of performance-based rewards.

Two important points must first be discussed concerning performance-based rewards. First, bonus plans have been proven to do a better job of motivating team members than skill-based pay raises. Second, team members assign higher credibility to objective performance measures based upon team achievements.[15] Therefore, global organizations that can tie rewards to quantifiable measures can more effectively change team member behavior to shift from an individual focus to a team focus than organizations that take a more subjective approach such as utilizing a manager's rating system.

The challenge in using performance-based reward systems for a global project or program team comes from the fact that the reward system has to be specifically designed to support a particular team. The team reward system must use measures and metrics that demonstrate successful team performance and tie the rewards to the achievement of the project or program goals.

An additional challenge is the timing of the rewards. The most common practice for rewarding team performance is to give bonuses to the team members at the conclusion of the project or program. However, as is often the case, the membership of the team changes throughout the duration of the project or program. Therefore it becomes difficult to gauge the appropriate contribution and resulting reward for members who participate in but are not part of the effort at the conclusion. One approach that has been successfully applied to address this challenge is to implement a phased approach to giving rewards. As the team members achieve the goals through the various phases of the project or program, incremental bonuses are given to the team members that participated in each particular phase.

Management Rewards

Recognition and rewards for senior and middle managers offer challenges as well. Specifically, we are referring here to the organizational managers who provide resources and other support and services to the global project and program teams. The rewards and recognition model shifts significantly as the organization transitions toward a horizontal collaborative approach. As we have discussed in earlier chapters, one of the key characteristics of the horizontal collaborative approach is one of driving projects and decision making transitions from the organizational managers to the global project or program team leader.

Senior managers must evaluate their individual organizational managers based upon the shift to the new model. Functional managers should not only be rewarded for their efforts in building a strong functional team, but also for their role in supporting the global project and program teams. Specifically, rewards should be based upon how well they provide mentoring and coaching, if they help remove obstacles, provide creative input, and guide the skills development of the team members – all of which lead to organizational value and long-term success. Global project and program team leaders should have the opportunity to provide performance feedback for the functional managers.

Senior managers should be evaluated and rewarded on how well the organization has transitioned to a globally-distributed team model. The critical role for senior managers is to design an organization that effectively operates in the global environment, and then to pay careful attention to establishing the opportunities for global teams to successfully perform.[16] This also includes, of course, ensuring that the rewards and recognition for organizational managers are properly aligned and administered in order to contribute to the success of the global teams.

Looking Ahead

Becoming a global leader within an industry takes time and continual investment. In this chapter, we looked at the primary organizational elements that leading global companies have focused upon to establish and maintain their leadership position by effectively executing their global strategies.

Up to this point, we have pointed out that the people achieving the most success in leading global teams possess a set of skills that separate them from other, less successful team leaders. In the next chapter, we delve into the details of the critical skills that go beyond the most common core leadership skills necessary for leading global teams by utilizing a core competency model to detail the knowledge, skills, and abilities needed for an experienced global project or program team leader to successfully perform his or her role.

CHAPTER SIX

Developing the Global Team Leader

"A leader is one who knows the way, goes the way and shows the way."
- John C. Maxwell

As previously stated, it is a rare occasion when a global project or program team leader comes to the role fully qualified to fulfill all aspects of the broad and encompassing set of skills and competencies that can be needed for the job. The successful global team leader is constantly seeking to learn and broaden his or her knowledge and experience in order to take on more complex and critical work. Senior management in turn needs to create a positive learning environment in order to encourage their global team leaders to continually seek improvement and growth.

In this chapter we use the Global Team Leader Competency Model to detail the knowledge, skills, and abilities needed for an experienced global project or program team leader to successfully perform his or her role. Additionally, we discuss the key organizational enablers needed to make the competency model fully effective, and to adequately support the global team leaders. Enablers are things that create or proactively encourage a positive environment to provide the maximum opportunity for success, learning, and growth to occur. Enablers range from environmental factors to organizational and managerial culture, philosophy, and actions.

With this chapter, we aim to assist all members of an organization to understand what core competencies are needed for the experienced and successful global team leader, the value of the competency set to the individual and the organization, and how the competency model can be used as a tool for career growth and performance evaluation of the global project or program team leader.

The Global Team Leader Competency Model

Global team leaders are *change agents*. Their programs and projects move the status quo within organizations from point "A" to point "B" or what is sometimes referred to as current state to future state. This requires a broad-based skill set that goes beyond traditional management. Noel Tichy, a noted scholar and author, claims that while management knowledge and skills in the areas of finance, manufacturing, and marketing are important to organizational success, they are woefully insufficient for effectively planning and sustaining organizational change and transformational initiatives.

The new level of responsibility and accountability granted to global project and program leaders as described above clearly requires a skill set and level of competency that is much higher than the traditional project manager who is many times put into the role of leading a global product or service development team. Successful global team leadership demands a skill set that includes business and financial acumen, an understanding of the products, services and customers served, and proven evidence that they possess the leadership and "soft" skills necessary to effectively manage complex development efforts in a highly distributed team across the global environment.

Possessing the right skills to lead in a global environment is necessary but not sufficient, however. Global team leaders must also be highly-competent individuals. Competence is defined as the knowledge, skills, and qualities of managers used to effectively perform the functions associated with management in the work situation.[1] A simple algorithm sums it up the best:

Competence = Knowledge + Skills + Personal Qualities + Experience

The Global Team Leader Competency Model (Figure 6-1) has been designed to provide the necessary knowledge, skills, and organizational enablers to systematically support the recruiting, staffing, professional development, and career planning of the global project or program team leader. The information presented in this section has been derived from companies that execute effectively in a global and highly-distributed environment. These companies have devised comprehensive training and development approaches to support this key role. Although the technical aspects of product and service development are critically important, much of the success of a global project or program is behavioral and human-oriented.

Figure 6-1: Global Team Leader Competency Model

One aspect that is worth pointing out from the summary view of the core competency areas of global team management is that project management is but one element of the competencies needed. One can visualize from Figure 6-1 that global team leadership is a much broader role than basic project management. In addition to strong project management competencies, the successful global project or program team leader needs to gain proficiency in global business, virtual team management, market, and leadership competencies. Without this added proficiency, the transition from a basic project management role to a global team leadership role is many times frustrating for the individual, the organization, and the customer.

Team Leadership Competencies

Leadership competencies are how we describe the "people skills" global team leaders need to be successful in leading a team of people and managing a set of stakeholders. As Max Dupree points out in his book titled *Leadership is an Art*, "Leadership is an art, something to be learned over time, not simply by reading books. The signs of outstanding leadership appear primarily among the followers. Are the followers reaching their potential? Are they learning? Are they achieving their objectives?"[2]

Figure 6-2: Team leadership skills

Specifically, we are referring to team leadership skills as outlined in Figure 6-2. The ability to lead the cross-organizational, cross-geographical, and cross-cultural team is a key role of the global project or program leader. The global team leader needs to have the capability to build, coalesce and champion the team to achieve product or service solutions that will satisfy the company's customers. The core leadership competencies of the global team leader fall in two categories: general leadership skills that are extended to leading a highly-distributed and multi-cultural team; and specific global team leadership skills, that when possessed by the team leader, significantly raise the probability of success in the global environment.

General Leadership Skills

As pointed out in Chapter Four, the foundational elements of effective team leadership apply whether one is leading a domestic team that is co-located in a single site, or a global team that is distributed across multiple sites and geographies. Success begins with the core principles of team leadership, and then an understanding of how to extend these leadership principles for application in a distributed team environment. The core principles of team leadership are as follows:

- Creating a common purpose
- Establishing team chemistry
- Building and sustaining trust
- Demonstrating personal integrity
- Empowering the team
- Driving participation, collaboration, and integration
- Communicating effectively
- Managing team conflict

- Making tough decisions
- Providing recognition and rewards

We refer the reader to Chapter Four where we explain each of the core team leadership skills in detail and explain how to apply each of them to effectively lead a globally-distributed team.

Global Team Leadership Skills

In addition to the core leadership skills, there are several important leadership skills that need special attention and further characterization due to their over-riding importance to the virtual team environment. These include influencing skills, prioritization skills, symphonic and systems skills, and political savvy.

Influencing skills. In the global team environment, members of the team rarely report directly to the project or program team leader. This requires that the team leader become proficient in influencing the actions of the team members. Additionally, influencing skills are required to positively affect the actions and decisions on the part of the senior management team, key partners and suppliers, and support organizations. As John Maxwell states in *The 21 Irrefutable Laws of Leadership*, "Leadership is influence – nothing more, nothing less. If you don't have influence, you will never be able to lead others."[3]

Successful influencing involves gaining support for your team when needed, inspiring others to do their best, persuading others to follow your direction and coalesce around a common team purpose, and creating strong relationships. It is about moving things forward without pushing, forcing, coercing, or threatening. Influencing traits of a strong global team leader include being socially adept in interacting with others in any given situation, having the ability to assess all aspects of information and behavior without passing judgment or injecting bias, and being able to effectively communicate your point of view to change opinion or change course of action.

Prioritization skills. The global team leader's ability to set and balance team priorities is one of the key indicators of success. The first step in setting priorities is checking to make sure the assumptions driving the project or program priorities are correct. It is one thing for the team leader to set the priorities, but it is most important to validate the priorities with the primary sponsors of the project or program. If the assumptions behind the priorities are incorrect, it is quite possible the priorities themselves will be incorrect. Once the priorities are validated, the global team leader should manage to the priorities. For example, if cost containment is the highest priority of the project or program, then the team leader must be emphatic about staying within the financial constraints. If technological leadership is the highest priority, the team leader will need to keep the team focused on the technical aspects of the project or program, and provide the necessary resources to ensure technological success.

Symphonic and systems skills. Symphonic skills involve obtaining balance and optimization across a multitude of diverse but related elements. In other words, it represents putting the pieces together harmoniously, resulting in a synergistic improvement. The ability to see the big picture, crossing boundaries, being able to combine disparate elements into a new holistic entity, and to see relationships between unrelated fields and broad patterns are characteristics of symphonic skills. Usually this ability resides in people with very wide backgrounds, multi-disciplined minds, and a broad spectrum of experiences.

Symphonic and systems skills also include the ability to see relationships between relationships, which goes by many names including systems, gestalt, and holistic thinking.4 Peter Senge effectively presented systems thinking as a framework from which one can organize and understand events, behaviors and phenomenon that affect one another in the short and long term. When one applies systems thinking as opposed to linear thinking, one can see the dynamics that are reinforcing an event or limiting growth.[5]

As described in Chapter Three, a system is a collection of parts or sub-systems that can be combined into an integrated whole to achieve an objective or entity. A functioning integrated whole is key to the definition. For example, a bicycle is a functioning system. However, if you remove the handlebars, it no longer is a functioning bicycle. Those skilled in systems thinking can view projects and activities from a broad perspective that includes seeing overall characteristics and patterns rather than just individual elements. By focusing on the entirety of the project, or in essence, the system aspects of the project (inputs, outputs, and interrelationships), the global team leader improves the probability of achieving the practical end solution and expectations of the intended customer.

Political savvy. Organizational politics originate when individuals drive their personal agendas and priorities at the expense of a cohesive corporate agenda. Company politics are a natural part of any organization, and the global team leader should understand that politics are a behavioral aspect of leading that he or she must contend with in order to succeed. The basis of organizational politics is really two-fold: one's desire to advance within the firm, and one's quest for power (usually in the form of controlling decisions and resources).[6]

The global team leader must actively manage the politics surrounding his or her project or program to protect against negative affects of political maneuvering on the part of stakeholders and to exploit politically-advantageous situations. In order to do this, it is important that the team leader possess both a keen understanding of the organization, and the political savvy necessary to build strong relationships to effectively leverage and influence the power base of the company.

The most effective method for managing in the organization's political environment is to leverage the project or program stakeholders and powerful members of one's network who can help achieve the project or program objectives.[7] The key is to avoid naivete, and understand that not every stakeholder sees great value in the project or program. From our experience, the global team leader who practices effective stakeholder management generates a greater probability of success. Stakeholders come to the table with a variety of expectations, demands, personal goals, agendas, and priorities that many times are in conflict with one another. The successful global team leader must rationalize and resolve these competing requirements by striking an appropriate balance between stakeholder's expectations and the realities of the project or program. A team leader, therefore, must be politically astute by being sensitive to the interests of the most powerful stakeholders, and at the same time, demonstrate good judgment by acting with integrity.[8]

Virtual Management Competencies

The positive impact by the team leader on members of the team has considerable merit especially when one considers that very few, if any, of the virtual team members report directly to the team leader. Achieving synergism in the virtual team setting as well as providing growth and development of the leader's team members during the life of the project is a significant accomplishment. Global team leadership challenges a leader well beyond what traditionally has been expected of team leaders in the past.

Described below are some of the more critical virtual team management skills that when possessed by the team leader, significantly raises their proficiency in leading globally-distributed teams. As highlighted in Figure 6-3, these include cross-cultural management, virtual communication, facilitation, networking, emotional intelligence, and contextual intelligence skills.

Figure 6-3: Virtual management skills

Cross-Cultural Management

Competence at cross-cultural management is critical in leading teams in the globally-distributed environment. Cross-cultural management is the ability to understand the behavior of people within diverse nations and cultures. It includes awareness of cultures you are directly involved in and understanding attitudes, differences, and behaviors. Its focus is toward improving the interaction and working relationship between team members, management, and suppliers from all the cultures represented in the direct and broader team. It requires us to examine our own biases and prejudices, develop cross-cultural skills, and when possible, observe and learn from culturally-proficient role models.

It is important to note that relative to leadership skills and style, one approach may work in one culture, but not work in another. According to Nancy Adler, "Some researchers suggest that American approaches to leadership apply equally well abroad. However, most believe that leaders must adapt their style and approach to the cultures of the involved employees and clients. That is, they believe that leadership is culturally contingent."[9]

The culturally-skilled global team leader is also adept at being sensitive to the following as it relates to observed actions and behaviors in various cultures:

- Listening for hidden communications in voice intonation and looking for non-verbal cues relative to facial expression, behavior and physical movement;

- Watching for the blinders to cultural sensitivity in themselves and team members such as stereotyping and projected similarity; and

- Studying their team members and interpreting each of their specific cultural biases as they pertain to power distance, uncertainty avoidance, level of context, and perceptions of career success and quality of life.

Only through understanding and appreciating the unique characteristics of their culture can the team leader show the proper level of respect and understanding that each team member deserves. This is not easy and few of us ever obtain a complete level of understanding. However, this should not prevent us as team leaders from making our best effort to sharpen our cultural skills, awareness, and behavior.

Virtual Communication Skills

Communicating virtually requires us to broaden our perspective and appreciation for the entire communication process due to the comprehensive set of challenges facing the exchange of meaning in a globally-distributed environment. Communication is any behavior another person perceives and interprets as the understanding of what was meant. Communication includes sending both verbal messages (words) and non-verbal messages (tone of voice, facial expressions, behaviors). It includes consciously sent messages as well as subtle messages that the sender is totally unaware of having sent. Communication therefore involves a complex multi-layered and dynamic process through which we exchange meaning.[10]

Communication on a globally-distributed team is complicated by the physical separation of team members and the resulting reliance upon technologies to facilitate team communication. The global team leader needs to develop skills in selecting the appropriate communication technologies given the tasks required, technical competence of the team members, and infrastructure capabilities within the geographies that team members reside.

The global team leader must then become proficient in the use of communication technologies selected to the level at which he or she can teach other team members how to use it as well as the appropriate communication etiquette associated with a technology. Electronic mail has become the dominant communication method for virtually-distributed teams because of convenience. However, miscommunication stories abound because of poor email usage. Jose Campos of RapidInnovation provides some sound advice on effective email usage in "Effective Email Practices for Global Teams."

Effective Email Practices for Global Teams

Contributed by Jose Campos

As our professional communities become more global, we find we often work with people who are in far-flung places, at least far from where we are. This means we will be communicating with team mates who don't share the same first language as us or the same cultural norms as us. We therefore need to develop more effective "global communication" skills so that we consistently deliver business results — even when the rest of our team or organization is scattered across the globe.

Collaboration using email is one way virtual business is conducted, but it comes with the following limitations which you may have encountered:

- How many times have you been unclear about the action you, personally, were expected to take after reading an email?

- How many times have you read an email with misspellings, missing words, or a grammatical error that obscured the sender's meaning?

- How do you know that an email message you send will be interpreted the proper way by someone whose language and culture are very different than yours?

- How many emails did it take to clarify an issue with your peers in other countries and for whom English is a second language?

Email is convenient. We can store it, delete it, and react to it instantly. Yet it is the immediacy of email that leads to the problems above if email is sent without thinking deeply about what has been written, and without checking for errors, expectations, outcomes and completeness.

Above all it is the clear understanding that words alone constitute only about 10 percent of overall communication, the rest is made up of facial expressions, body language, tone and other physical manifestations; therefore, email starts with a handicap as it only contains words — you are in effect sending only 10 percent of the communication.

What to do

The following are 11 suggestions for improving the quality and consistency of business email in a distributed environment:

1. Write and send with care. Email is a very casual mode of communication, and we often choose to use it to discuss critical issues. When we do, it is critical to read and write with the importance and focus that the issue deserves. Focus your attention to ensure that you give the message your full concentration.

2. Take full advantage of the subject line. The subject line should give a clear idea of content and action needed. When sending a reply, change the subject line if it needs changing, do not just drag out an old email from weeks ago and re-use it to cover a new topic without changing what the subject line says. And, whatever you do, do not send the message in the "subject" line as the limited characters

available do not provide adequate context for the reader.

3. Cover one item of business in each email message. For distributed teams, emails have replaced the printed memo as announcement, reminder, and call to action. Use separate messages with individual subject headings to make it easier for the reader, allowing them to understand, review, and react to each subject logically.

4. Clarify what actions are required of each recipient. Ambiguity of actions required can cost the virtual team precious time. Remember that an action item is made up of three parts: 1) do what, 2) by whom, 3) by when – for example, "John, please develop a database of all Midwestern customers by the end of this week. I will need the database by Wed., Nov. 16, at 2 pm EST." - anything less than that and it is not an action item.

5. Be wary of emotionally-charged content. If you have something emotional to share, it is best to do it in person or on the phone. Understanding is gained through voice, body language, and facial expressions. Too many people use email as a shield to avoid unpleasant confrontations, and they end up alienating the recipient. If you would not say something to someone in person, do not say it in an email.

6. Do not use email to deliver the really bad news. Never use email to chastise or criticize, and never (never!) to deliver any seriously bad

news. A message that may seem reasonable to you can hit another person hard, and you will not know it since you cannot see the reader's nonverbal cues. Any message that will have a major effect on an employee's work or life should be delivered face to face or at least over the phone.

7. Apply a professional demeanor. Minimize the use of underlines, boldface, all caps, and exclamation points. These all have the same unpleasant effect as shouting at someone face to face.

8. Acknowledge receipt and respond promptly. In many cases, the sender is waiting for a reply from you; even it is just an acknowledgement that you received the message. Consider that things may be "on hold" until you reply, which can impact productivity and decision making. When you receive a request or an action item, take immediate action. For example, if someone is asking for a meeting date, let him or her know immediately of your availability or alternatives.

9. Be judicious in your use of group addresses. There may well be no need to copy all 47 members of the team on every memo. This decreases our team mates' productivity and often leads people to assume "someone else will handle it." The hope is that someone else among those 47 people will do it, so "I don't have to."

10. Read and edit before you send. As a form of written communication, email represents you professionally. Send your best. And for particularly important messages or any message composed in anger, treat your message as if it were a traditional letter: write, print, read, revise, and then send. And remember; never send an email without first checking the spelling. Typos and other blemishes make the message difficult to read.

11. Do not send or read email at inappropriate times. Email has become an addiction, but the constant pursuit of an email fix may be costly. One of the newer forms of poor office etiquette is paying more attention to email than to a conversation or business meeting. It has been proven that if a person is attending to multiple things at the same time, they are not going to retain as much information and will make more errors than if they were focusing on one thing. This can lead to lost productivity and wasted dollars because people are not focused on their work. It is best practice to dedicate periods of time during the day when one can read and respond to email as a single task.

Let's face it. Email is a convenient, fast, and valuable tool in the distributed team and virtual business environment. Like any tool, it can facilitate or hinder communication. Used effectively and in concert with face-to-face meetings, email is an exceptional way to share information, foster creative thinking, and facilitate critical personal meetings.

Facilitation Skills

Simply put, facilitation is the act of assisting team members to reach their collective goals by helping to make team communication and collaboration easier and more effective. Good facilitation skills help to ensure that relationships between team members continue to develop and that ongoing communication and collaboration between team members is occurring as needed. Facilitation skills needed in a virtual environment go well beyond those needed for domestic teams.

Communication and collaboration in a virtual team environment does not occur spontaneously at the onset of a global project or program, even if team members are familiar with one another and have previously worked together. The geographic and time separation between team members creates communication and collaboration challenges. Co-located team members have an advantage over their globally-distributed counterparts because they have the opportunity for spontaneous conversations and collaboration enabled by the work environment. To complicate matters more, national, organizational, and functional differences between global team members create natural communication and collaboration barriers. Global team leaders must, therefore, utilize facilitation skills to overcome the time, distance, and cultural barriers to stimulate and sustain effective virtual communication and collaboration within their teams.

Many aspects of successful leadership of a global project or program team covered in this text rely on collective communication and collaboration between team members. Specifically, they rely on strong facilitation skills on the part of the global team leader to guide the necessary collective communication and collaboration between team members to perform the following:

- Crafting the project or program vision and common purpose;

- Establishing the team norms;
- Creating the team charter;
- Solving project or program-related problems;
- Building strong personal relationships;
- Reaching good decisions;
- Managing conflict between team members;
- Identifying and managing cross-team deliverables;
- Brainstorming new ideas; and
- Enforcing team rules.

Each aspect of global team leadership identified above is critical to project or program success, and each requires facilitated discussion and collaboration between the global team members. It is the global team leader who must provide the facilitation leadership.

Core facilitation skills include the ability to draw out varying opinions and viewpoints among team members, to create a discussion and collaboration framework consisting of a clear end state and discussion and collaboration boundaries, to summarize and to synthesize details into useful information and strategy, and to lead the adoption of technological communication and collaboration tools. Other facilitation skills which are beneficial include using personal energy to maintain forward momentum, being able to rationalize cause and effect, helping team members to establish one-on-one relationships, keeping team members focused on the primary topics of discussion and collaboration, and demonstrating the ability to deliver an effective presentation.

Arguably, the most critical facilitation skill is a global team leader's ability to lead virtual meetings. Since majority significant amount of communication and collaboration between team members occurs in team meetings, the global team leader has to develop skills in planning and conducting remote meetings. Virtual team meetings will run the gamut from face-to-face meetings, phone conferences, video conferences, internet-based data sharing meetings, or some combination of all of these. This involves pre-planning an agenda with time-boxed topics, sending any materials that will be used in the meeting to all members prior to the meeting, setting the meeting ground rules, facilitating the discussion appropriately to ensure a mutual understanding of all conversations, and periodically checking to see if quiet members are understanding the discussion and are fully engaged.

Utilization of the various technical tools available should enhance good facilitation practices by enabling team members to share concepts, merge information, and formulate new ideas. Technological tools, however, will not make up for poor and improperly facilitated meetings.[11] It is the project or program leader's responsibility to facilitate *effectiveness* and rely on technology tools for *efficiency*.

Networking Skills

One's ability to network successfully across worldwide hierarchical and organizational boundaries is a tremendously useful skill given that customers, senior managers, team members, and other critical parties are dispersed across multiple distances, sites, and countries in a global product or service development effort.

The global team leader first must know how to determine the organizational landscape and who is in it. This involves effective stakeholder identification and political mapping capabilities. He or she must then be able to use and extend this knowledge to develop the ability to choose the right mode of communication to address customers, senior management, team members, suppliers, and others. This involves knowing when to see people face-to-face, when to send messages, and when to avoid them altogether.

Networking also involves becoming skilled in decision making by knowing how to determine the right parties to be involved in project or program decisions, understanding the impacts of a decision, and developing the appropriate messaging for the decision at hand. Before driving for a decision, good networking skills require a global team leader to ask four essential questions:[12]

1. What do the stakeholders have to lose by this decision?

2. Does the decision change the organizational power structure?

3. How would I react to this decision if it were presented to me?

4. Is the material, concept, and decision criteria clear and easy to understand?

This, in most cases, creates the need for what Daniel Pink (author of "A Whole New Mind) defines as *complex communications* which entail persuading, explaining, and in other ways, conveying a particular interpretation of information.[13]

From a team perspective, effective networking skills gives the global team leader the ability to create a sense of urgency in team members who are potentially isolated at great distance from the rest of the team or are being pulled toward other competing priorities. They also enable team members to adapt to the virtual, cross-national environment, and positively encourage the team members to work outside their normal comfort zone.

Emotional Intelligence Skills

There exists a strong argument that the Intelligence Quotient (IQ), which traditionally has been the measure of intelligence, ignores key behavioral and personality elements. Beyond IQ, success depends upon the awareness, control, and management of our own emotions and those of others around us, which forms the basis of the concept of Emotional Intelligence (EI).

As global companies have searched for the most critical leadership competencies, they have learned that emotional intelligence, not cognitive abilities, contributes to as much as 90% of the differences between star performers and average performers.[14] Additionally, research by the Center of Creative Leadership found that the primary causes of derailment in executives involve deficits in emotional competence such as difficulty in handling change, not being able to work well in a team, and poor interpersonal relations.[15]

Daniel Goleman describes emotional intelligence as "managing with heart."[16] His ground breaking book, *Emotional Intelligence* redefines what it means to be competent as a leader. EI skills are especially critical in a globally-distributed team environment due to the lack of regular face-to-face interaction and involvement, a higher level of complexity, and the cross-cultural nature of the work. Being acutely in tune and sensitive to emotions and emotional responses of both the leader and his or her team members is critical to success of a development effort. According to Travis Bradberry and Jean Greaves, emotional intelligence is the single biggest predictor of performance in the workplace and the strongest driver of leadership and personal excellence. Emotional intelligence skills are more important to job performance than any other leadership skill.[17]

Emotional intelligence skills consist of two types of competencies: personal competence and social competence. Personal competence involves both self awareness and self management, where self awareness is one's ability to accurately perceive one's own emotions and moods in the moment and understand one's tendencies in various situations. Self management is the ability to use awareness of emotions to stay flexible and direct one's behavior positively. Thus, self awareness involves staying on top of one's reactions to team members and others and managing one's own emotional self regulation to think before one acts or reacts.

Social competence includes social awareness and relationship management skills that drive at understanding others and managing relationships. Social awareness is one's ability to accurately pick up on the emotions of others and to understand what is really going on with them whether one agrees with them or not. In essence, it is applying empathy and appropriately understanding and reacting to the emotional needs of others.

Relationship management is the ability to use personal competence and social competence to recognize both one's own emotions and those of others to manage interactions successfully. This forms the foundation for the bonding and building of long-term personal relationships over time.

Contextual Intelligence Skills

The contextual environment in which leaders operate within the global setting is increasingly complex. The environment is continually evolving and is both dynamic and turbulent. Decisions must be made quickly and must be effectively useful and practical. Leaders able to perform successfully given these challenges have a high degree of contextual intelligence.

Context is the setting in which events occur. It consists of internal and external factors surrounding the circumstances of the event and the application of the leader's intelligence to transform the data into useful information. Mathew R. Kutz, author of *Contextual Intelligence: An Emerging Competency For Global Leaders*, defines contextual intelligence as "the ability to quickly and intuitively recognize and diagnose the dynamic contextual variables inherent in an event or circumstance, which results in intentional adjustment of behavior in order to exert appropriate influence in that context."[18] It results in integrating and diagnosing information while exercising and applying knowledge pertinent to the contextual situation.

Contextual intelligence skills are "an innate ability to synthesize information quickly and effectively" note researchers Erik Dane and Michael Pratt.[19] It also means being astute at detecting attitudes, motivation and resistance of vested parties involved in a specific event or project effort. Team leaders who possess a high degree of contextual intelligence are able to cognitively and intuitively assimilate the various data and observations surrounding an event and effectively turn that into information useful to making decisions.

Global Business Competencies

In most cases, the responsibility for managing the business for the global project or program falls upon the global team leader, not the business unit manager. In effect, the global team leader operates as the business unit manager's proxy, responsible for achieving the business objectives and results intended from the product or service development endeavor. Strong business competencies are required to fulfill this role, including the ability to develop a comprehensive project or program business case that supports the company's objectives and strategies, the ability to manage within the business aspects of the company, and the ability to understand and analyze the related financial measures pertaining to the product or service under development (see Figure 6-4).[20]

Figure 6-4: Global business skills

Business Fundamental skills

To be successful from a business perspective, the global project or program team leader must possess sufficient business skills to understand the organization's business model and financial goals, utilizing economic, financial, and organizational data to build and document the business case for their project or program, and being proficient in business terminology when communicating with senior managers and other business-minded stakeholders.

This requires the global team leader to have a working knowledge and level of proficiency in business fundamentals including capabilities in financial analysis and accounting, international management, political issues, law and ethics, resource management, negotiation and communication, and management of intellectual property. Additionally, it may be required that the team leader possess a working knowledge of the local and international economics in which the project or program is operating.

Strategic Thinking Skills

The global team leader is required to think strategically in order to align the project or program to the strategic objectives of the organization. A part of strategic thinking involves a basic understanding of the industry in which the business operates. Industry trends, knowledge about competitors, and supply chain implications are a fundamental part of keeping a project or program viable from a business perspective.

World View Skills

Being proficient in global business also means possessing a world view. As stated in Chapter One, a world view refers to developing an awareness of the global environment to include social, political, and economic trends. The global team leader must be able to apply his or her knowledge, skills and competencies within the global business context.

Present in a world view is the fact that globalization is driven by a set of forces that have operated interdependently throughout recent history. Knowledge of the three primary globalization forces – economic forces, political forces, and technology forces – provides senior managers and global team leaders with a greater contextual understanding of the environment in which they operate. The world view capability is, of course, significantly enhanced through an individual's experience and exposure to various international markets and cultures.

Customer and Market Competencies

Customer and market competency involves having a thorough understanding of the market in which the product or service is being sold, and how it will be used by the customer and end user. The better the global team leader and his or her team can closely align the product or service with the customer's needs, the more it will enhance the potential for customer satisfaction and the successful achievement of the business results intended. Figure 6-5 highlights the critical skills involved in the customer and market competency area.

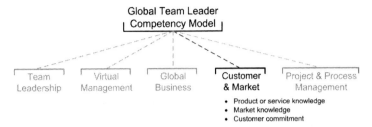

Figure 6-5: Customer and market knowledge areas

Product or service knowledge

At a minimum level, the global project or program team leader must understand the customer's needs and desires that are pertinent to the new product or service under development. This requires sufficient technical knowledge to understand how the needs can be met by the product or service, and how to integrate the elements of the design and development into a successful and appropriate solution for the customer.

Market knowledge

As a company expands globally, its customer base and the markets it sells in or serves become more diverse. This may require the global team leader to embark on a continual learning path to stay abreast of various markets. This does not mean to imply that the global team leader needs to be the customer, market, and industry expert on the team. This would most likely consume most, if not all, of his or her time and energy. Rather, the global team leader must know how to tap in to this type of expertise within the enterprise to maintain a general level of knowledge and to bring pertinent information to the global team.

Customer commitment

The global team leader must be the consummate customer advocate for the project or program that he or she leads. This means being skilled in *voice of the customer* techniques to ensure the needs and desires of the customer are reflected in the final product or service. Customer advocacy also means that customer quality is a fundamental element of success of the overall project or program. This requires an understanding of how customer quality is defined, how it should be measured, and then keeping the entire team and stakeholders focused on achieving the quality targets that define quality success.

Project and Process Management Competencies

The final element of the Global Team Leader Competency Model is project and process management as illustrated in Figure 6-6. The global team leader should be well versed in the core development processes of the firm as well as basic project management processes, methods, and tools to effectively manage the tactical elements of the global project or program.

Figure 6-6: Process and project management skills

The team leader that develops this competency will increase his or her probability of gaining team member's confidence and trust. They will become confident that their leader knows how to get things done in a timely and successful manner.

Process proficiency

An important aspect of this core skill set is that of becoming proficient at possessing a solid working knowledge of the specific processes and practices of the company. Knowing how things get done, the policies and procedures that must be adhered to, and who must be involved and approve various aspects of the development effort are critical for the successful completion of every project or program. If it is a product-based company, for example, the team leader must be thoroughly familiar with the firm's new product design, development, and market launch process to insure that the development team and effort adheres to management's requirements and expectations as to how products are designed and built.

Lifecycle Management Skills

A challenge in leading a global team becomes one of ensuring that all members of the team are consistently following the same processes and methods, and are using the same tools when appropriate. A foundational element in driving process consistency across the global team is to ensure that a common lifecycle is being used by all. This will help to drive common language and terminology, establish a common cadence of activities, and provide common decision and synchronization points throughout the product or service development cycle.

Project Management Skills

In addition to being skilled in the core project management competencies required by the methodology used (Agile or PRINCE2 for example), the global team leader must become proficient in knowing how to apply the elements of a particular methodology in a highly-distributed team environment. For example, communication management is a core competency area for any of the project management methodologies. However, none of the methodologies today describes how to effectively manage communication in a virtual team environment using various electronic communication technologies. This knowledge has to be gained outside of the core project management methodologies. The same can be said for all the core project management competency areas.

Stakeholder Management Skills

Stakeholder management is a skill that is critical to global project or program management success. The global team leader can have many stakeholders that he or she has to manage both internal and external to the organization. Effective stakeholder management helps the team leader gain cooperation from the highly influential stakeholders, cut through competing stakeholder agendas, and confront stakeholders that may be inhibiting progress. Good stakeholder management first of all involves understanding who the stakeholders are and their needs, understanding the level of influence each stakeholder has on the project or program, and understanding their allegiance and attitude toward the project or program (never assume all stakeholders want the effort to succeed). From this information, the global team leader can determine which stakeholders he or she needs to manage and how to manage them.

Finally, competence is increased with experience. Global project and program team leaders cannot gain the necessary expertise by learning in a classroom or from reading a book. The role needs to be practiced. Improvement comes with a history of successes and failures associated with actually leading global teams and true evidence of competence comes from a track record of proven accomplishments that represents an individual's experience base. We know that all global team leaders do not come to their respective roles fully qualified. They need to be trained and grow into these roles through accomplished experience.

As Malcolm Gladwell teaches us, "The idea that excellence at performing a complex task requires a critical minimum level of practice surfaces again and again in studies of expertise. The emerging picture from such studies is that a considerable amount of time is required to achieve the level of mastery associated with being a world-class expert in anything".[21]

Global Team Leader Staffing and Performance Evaluation

The ability to select the best candidates available for the global team leader role will enhance the organization's ability to achieve its global execution objectives. Assuming the firm may have multiple levels of global team leaders needed, job descriptions can be tailored to fit each position. These positions may range from entry level global team leaders that are to lead smaller, less complex efforts to senior global team leaders for the larger, more complex efforts. Once the global team leader job description is characterized and includes the knowledge, skills and abilities required for the role, it can serve as the basis for establishing the screening, selection and hiring criteria. Positions can be filled either through qualified new hires or by selecting individuals within the firm that possess the potential to grow into the role.

The global team leader job description can also serve as the basis for individual performance evaluation. The job description, project or program objectives, and expectations by management will serve as the basis for determining and documenting the accomplishments and overall performance of the individual team leader.

The global team leader job descriptions and corresponding pay levels, once approved and implemented, can serve as the basis for each team leader's periodic (normally annual) performance setting and appraisal process. Performance evaluations, when done correctly, can provide appropriate recognition for better performance, increased personal motivation, as well as for course correction for performance misses. The performance evaluation, coupled with the use of the Global Team Leader Competency Model for identifying training and development opportunities for a specific team leader can become a powerful process for driving continual improvement in the performance of the firm's global team leaders and potentially improve the overall business and operational results for the organization.

Global Team Leader Training and Professional Development

The knowledge, skills and abilities described as part of the Global Team Leader Competency Model are most useful for growing and developing the firm's team leaders. The Global Team Leader Competency Model can also be used as a tool or guideline for continual career development for the team leader. Ongoing dialogue between the individual team leader and his or her direct manager can be focused on understanding the team leader's growth and developmental needs. The result of these discussions, balanced with management's short and long range performance expectations for the individual, can be formulated into a development plan to support the individual for a given time period (usually one year). It is a process for the manager and the individual team leader to jointly target where they want the individual to be in his or her performance and career at some point in the future and then creating a development plan for how to get there. Future individual gains are made through a process of ongoing continual improvement and growth in skills and capability which, in turn, will lead to improvements in performance.

Training and development can be achieved through many different methods. Some individuals relate and respond better to certain modes of training than others. David Kolb, Howard Gardner, and other authors have published research on the dominant or preferred learning styles. These can be useful for assessing what approaches may work best for those seeking training. Kolb's cycle of learning provides insight into the learning process for each of us including experiencing, reflecting, thinking, and acting. "Immediate or concrete experiences lead to observations and reflections. These reflections are then assimilated (absorbed and translated) into abstract concepts with implications for action which the individual actively tests and experiments with, which in turn enables the creation of new experiences.[22]

To broaden a global team leader's capabilities to reach his or her full potential, it is helpful if senior management provides the means and encouragement for continual improvement in his or her discipline. Growth and improvement in the knowledge, skills, and abilities can be achieved through a combination of the following training and development sources:

- **Internal training courses.** Some firms offer their own training courses. They may be face-to-face classes or web-based.

- **External training seminars and courses.** A wealth of professional organizations and consulting firms offer a variety of courses pertinent to achieving elements and skills of the Global Team Leader Competency model.

- **College degree programs.** Several colleges and universities offer broad-based bachelor and masters level programs in project management and leadership.

- **Certifications.** Courses and certifications related to program and project management are offered through organizations such as the Project Management Institute and Product Development Management Association

- **Rotational assignments.** On-the-job training and experience within a firm is an effective technique for senior management to target the broadening of experience and capability of specific global team leaders.

- **Mentoring relationships.** Newer global team leaders can gain much knowledge, coaching and capability enhancement by being partnered with a mentor who is an experienced global team leader.

- **Communities of practice.** Many firms have effectively enriched and grown skills and capabilities through the use of communities of practice targeted at specific professional disciplines within their organization. A community of practice can be initiated and offered to all global team leaders in a firm in order to share best practices and engage them in skill enrichment exercises and ongoing learning activities.

Enablers for Global Team Leader Success

No amount of global team leader knowledge, skill, and experience can compensate for serious organizational barriers that impede global product and service development success. Even the most skilled and knowledgeable global team leaders will likely fail unless the barriers and impediments are appropriately addressed within an enterprise.

It is worth repeating that senior managers of an organization play a critical role in setting their global project and program team leaders up for success. This involves providing a proper foundation for global execution that aligns with the global strategies of the enterprise. Provided below is a summary of the top few critical *enablers* that have been described throughout this text that will increase the probability of global team leader success.

Enabler 1: Structure

An organizational structure that is aligned appropriately to enhance horizontal collaboration. In order to align the firm's globalization strategy and its execution output, senior management and the global team leaders must have direct access to each other to work together as a leadership team within a collaborative organizational structure.

Enabler 2: The Right Development Model

Adoption by senior management of a development model for execution that effectively supports the highly-distributed nature of the global environment. The development model needs to insure that execution output is directly linked to specific business goals, is sufficiently broad based to enable focus on a holistic development solution for the customer or client, and all dispersed elements are synchronized over the development lifecycle while employing a high degree of cross-organization, cross-functional collaboration.

Enabler 3: Empowerment

Team leaders that are formally empowered by senior management with the appropriate level of authority and decision responsibility pertinent to their role as the global team leaders. Transfer of power further enables the global team leaders to transfer appropriate decision-making capability to team members at the local level where the best information and knowledge about the project or program may exist.

Enabler 4: Processes

A set of product lifecycle procedures with appropriate decision checkpoints along with other pertinent company policies and procedures are established and consistently applied across all sites participating in the project or program. This will insure that all development effort worldwide is in compliance with all requirements and provides an effective means for mitigating business and operational risk.

Enabler 5: Tools

Appropriate electronic communication and collaboration tools are in place and available for virtual communication and collaboration across all vested team sites and geographies. These tools are supported by consistent procedures and team norms in order to optimize communication and the flow of information across all appropriate global sites.

Enabler 6: Formal Escalation Process

A process is in place that elevates barriers and issues outside the control of the team leader to senior management in order to get timely resolution. This also involves a system of documented success criteria, targets, and measures to indicate when escalation is needed and when it is not.

Enabler 7: Skills and Competencies

Team leader roles are staffed with individuals possessing the appropriate level of competence and experience to be successful in the globally-distributed team environment.

The level of responsibility and accountability granted to the global team leader requires a skill set that is much more comprehensive than the traditional project manager.

Enabler 8: Team Leader Growth

Recognition by senior management of the importance of continual growth and awareness of the need for increased competence in cross-cultural management for the firm. As it pertains to the leadership of teams, philosophies and behaviors, the blending of cultures must permeate through the organization.

Enabler 9: Rewards and Recognition

A global human resources management system is in place that appropriately addresses global needs. The human resource organization has implemented policies that are designed to support the international team participants and has reward and recognition systems that are balanced and equitable. This entails a comprehensive approach by the human resources department management that focuses on retaining key talent that goes beyond just monetary incentives to also include personal growth and job satisfaction.[23]

Enabler 10: Face-to-face Investment

Approval by senior management for at least one face-to-face meeting of all critical participants on new globally-distributed projects. This will contribute to building trust among team members that will form the foundation for their ongoing working relationships on the project and contribute to improved synergy and positive chemistry on the team.

Looking Ahead

As a firm begins to execute its product and service development efforts in a global environment, the leadership capability of its project and program team leaders becomes a critical component to success. Unfortunately, it is rare that the global team leader comes to his or her job fully qualified and capable to lead a highly-distributed, multi-cultural team. As evidenced by the Global

Team Leader Competency Model, the skills and competencies of the global team leader are vast and broad.

As one evaluates the skills, competencies and knowledge required of the global project or program team leader, as well as the organizational enablers that help to make him or her successful, it becomes clear that transitioning from a domestic product or service development environment to a global development environment will require organizational change.

In the next chapter, global project and program team leadership and organization transition change management are aligned. The difficulties of change associated with organizational culture, design, and management philosophy are described to illustrate the interdependencies of these management essentials.

CHAPTER SEVEN

Leading the Global Transition

"Start small, and grow steadily - be wary of giant first steps that take you places you're not ready to go."
- Peter Senge

Any organization that embarks on a globalization strategy sets itself on a path of significant organizational change. The companies that systematically manage change required to transition from a domestic environment to the global environment are the companies with the greatest probability of success. A manager from a leading global company told us that "Although organizational change can seem chaotic, success is really grounded in persistence, an understanding of what needs to be done for where you want to go, and an integrated framework or plan that serves as a roadmap to help you get there." Indeed, the lack of a systematic approach to organizational change is a common cause of failure for companies that take on a globalization strategy, but find that they cannot realize the business results intended by the strategy.

Based on the challenges associated with organizational change, you may think this is a new phenomenon, but there is nothing new about change. The pressures leading to organizational change have been forecasted for decades. What is new, however, is the pressure to plan for, lead, sustain, and adapt to globalization change is accelerating and thus causing significant challenge – future shock some may argue – within most organizations. Beyond Biblical change warned and led by the likes of Moses and Noah, and beyond the more recent major changes associated with the Industrial Revolution, significant warnings and ideas of change were offered by Alvin Toffler in his 1970 book, *Future Shock.*[1]

Toffler was convinced that change was becoming overwhelming for people due to technological and social pressures, which can leave people disconnected, suffering from stress, anxiety, and disorientation, or shock. Future shock, as he noted, is recognized as too much change in too short a period of time. He concluded that the majority of problems, especially social problems, were symptoms of future shock. Toffler did not realize that he was describing the effects globalization would cause several decades later.

While some award Moses with the title as the first organizational change agent,[2] it was Toffler's predications in the recent past that fueled the need for an acute focus on change – especially the human side of change within organizations.

Each decade following Toffler's future shock warnings has brought a new set of theorists, who repeatedly tell us that change is occurring at a rapid pace, and that change is difficult to navigate and manage. Here is a sample of organizational change theorist proclamations over the past several decades:

> Daryl Conner noted that "Never before has so much changed so fast and with such dramatic implications for the entire world. Life is transforming as we live it."[3]

John Kotter concluded that "By any objective measure, the amount of significant, often traumatic, change in organizations has grown tremendously over the past two decades."[4]

Wayne Casio noted that organizational change is occurring at a dramatic pace, much more so than in the past, and is likely to continue at a drastic pace into the foreseeable future.[5]

Peter Vaill described the changing environment in which we all operate and to which we contribute as "permanent white water" thus denoting it is difficult to predict and navigate.[6]

Peter Drucker suggested that "Major changes—both the major threats and the major opportunities—will dominate the executive's task in the next ten to fifteen years, maybe even longer."[7]

Frances Cairncross proclaimed that changes would grow faster in the next twenty-five years as compared to ever before. [8]

Karen Colteryahn and Patty Davis quantified the degree of change stating that the business world is changing at an unprecedented degree, doubling every ten years, which in turn causes uncertainty in economic conditions, organizational structures, globalization, workforce diversity, security concerns, and technology. [9]

These testaments provide outsiders' views of the realities being experienced by senior leaders and team leaders alike as their organizations execute their globalization strategies. None of the theorists, however, offers an integrated framework as the means to successfully plan, lead, and sustain organizational change and business transition from a domestic company to a global company.

In this chapter we review the types of change that need to be implemented within an organization that embarks on a globalization strategy, explain the organizational components that become impacted by the change, and provide insight into why people resist change and what can be done about it.

Organizational Dynamics and Successful Organizational Change

Niccolo Machiavelli noted that "there is nothing more difficult to take in hand, more perilous to conduct, or more uncertain in its success, than to take the lead in the introduction of a new order of things."[10] Anyone who has tried to institute a new procedure in the workplace, implement a new system, change the way that work is done for the benefit of the organization, or in our study here, go global, knows that change does not happen easily. Effective change is intentionally driven, carefully planned, and meticulously measured.

According to many researchers, 60 to 70 percent of organizational change initiatives fail to meet intended objectives.[11] A recent BusinessWeek study on global product and service development found that only 18 percent of the companies perceived their global product development programs to be very successful.[12] One of the members in our research sample noted a 90 percent organizational change failure rate within his company. Indeed, change, as driven by project, program, or product teams, is difficult, but as these statistics suggest, although effective change is improbable, it is not impossible.

Organizational change difficulty is in part due to the sheer number of components within an organization that need to undergo at least some change when a company begins to transition from being a domestic company to a global company. To demonstrate this point, let us look at some of the elements within an organization that may have to change as presented in previous chapters:

- A firm's organizational structure may have to be flattened to enable a higher degree of communication and collaboration across the company.

- A new development model may have to be adopted to facilitate the high degree of horizontal collaboration needed for global product or service development.

- The organizational culture may change to embrace new national, functional, and organizational cultures that have been acquired.

- Performance measurement, reward, and recognition systems may have to be modified.

- Training, development, and other help mechanisms may have to be modified to develop the new skills and competencies needed to lead in a global environment.

- Technologies may have to be added or changed to enable communication and collaboration in a virtual team setting.

Any *one* of the items above can involve a great deal of organizational change and often the change in one may impact another thus creating more change. Looked at collectively, one can see that globalization must be executed as an evolutionary process that requires a thoughtful, detailed, and carefully-executed transition management plan.

Companies who have failed or who are struggling in their global transition efforts often try to change too much, too soon. They also often fail to think through which elements of the organization must change, in what order, and fail to determine the interdependency impacts of one organizational component on another.

As all companies who embark on a globalization strategy learn, change is hard. But the demand for growth and the lure of globalization to achieve that growth are creating a growing need for organizations to implement major changes in order to respond competitively (and in some industries for sheer survival). So, the logical question is how do the global leaders – those who are embracing change and in some cases causing change for others – operate in the 30 percent margin of organizational change successes? Understanding the challenge of change is the first step in understanding how to become a master at change and operate on the success side of the ratio rather than on the failure side.

Before introducing an idealized list of critical components for successful organizational change, it is prudent to first review the fundamentals of organizational dynamics. It is commonly known that organizations are dynamic, but it is lesser known what the dynamics "look" like and what implications they have for one another. Many global companies know their supply chain and distribution channels. Fewer, however, are aware of the importance of understanding the implications of change in one component of the organization relative to another.

Due to the complexity of organizational change, especially when attempting to realize globalization efficiencies and effectiveness, the entire organization is impacted. Recent research uncovered the following categories that define the dynamics of a company.

People	Skills & Abilities	Performance
Tasks	Technology & Systems	Structure
Purpose	Help Mechanisms	Relationships
Leadership	Culture & Climate	Environment/ Context
Arrangements	Missions	Strategy
Process	Networks	Communication
Decision Making	Motivation	Practices

During our research and investigation into organizational change, members noted that the list itself is fine, but not very meaningful in simple list form. The understanding and meaning of the components and specifically the question "Why is it so difficult to lead successful organizational change initiatives?" was not truly understood until time was spent mapping the interdependencies of each component. This mapping resulted in the list above being categorized into six components of organizational dynamics. Importantly, the six components were arranged causally thus determining the impact one has on another. The notion of causal dynamics is illustrated in Figure 7-1 and allows us to "see" the relationship of each of these organizational components. This illustration represents the interdependencies of organizational work and the impact change has on an organization.

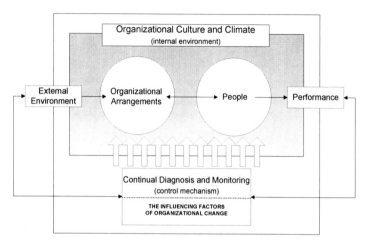

Figure 7-1: The dynamics of organizational work

Derek Ridmour explained to us that success in going global and sustaining global effectiveness is "All about metrics. Constant study and diagnosis of the market [external environment] and your operations [performance] is the key in achieving successful change, especially on a global scale."

We tend to agree with Ridmour's conclusion, which supports Figure 7-1. Diagnosing the conditions of the external environment and the performance of internal operations are three primary components for effective change. The other three components include organizational arrangements, people, and culture. Collectively, these capture the simple list of organizational dynamics and make greater sense of them relative to the causal model – any change in one has the potential to impact another thus causing more change. The way in which organizational arrangements and people work together creates the organization's performance, and diagnosing that performance relative to the external environment is collectively known as the way work gets done. This collection of components creates the organization's culture. Understanding this domestically is important. Understanding this globally is vital.

Diagnosing Global Performance

As illustrated in Figure 7-1, to effectively change an organization requires deliberate and continuous diagnosis of both external and internal pressures. Diagnosing the global environment includes the evaluation and analysis of product and service competition as well as geographic and organizational competitive advantages and disadvantages, customer requirements and trends, legislation and regulation, economic conditions on both a local and global scale, international politics, and social and cultural values. Global leaders, through the diagnosis of their external environment, coupled with the knowledge of Hofstede's work and their own organizational culture recognize the challenges associated with dispersing work globally and plan business transition for change accordingly.

Diagnosing internal performance is often thought of in terms of profit margins, market share, and operational efficiency ratios like time to market. While these are important, effective diagnostic work also includes measuring innovativeness relative to the needs and competition of the external environment, team cohesion, morale and satisfaction, and skill and knowledge. Effectively diagnosing these performance elements allows for perspective between targets and actual performance. The gaps between target and actual performance help determine the needed changes.

Essentially, the result from effective diagnosis is the uncovering of problems and opportunities for managers to address. Further, continuous diagnosis provides an on-going status of current-state situations. This status, coupled with trend analysis, offers the ability to envision what needs attention relative to problems and opportunities. Executing solutions to address problems and opportunities means change – incremental or radical, continuous or discontinuous. Effective change agents and global leaders recognize the value of continuous rather than discontinuous change and small, incremental change rather than radical change.

It is easy on a global scale to get overwhelmed and therefore it is important to address change in small step-by-incremental-step changes. This approach was recommended in Chapter Three regarding a globally-distributed product development model – disaggregate the whole into pieces that are manageable and measurable. Warren Bennis was one, among many that warned against initiating large, revolutionary change.[13] Based on our experience and research, we echo this sage advice.

Organizational change has some uniqueness to every organization. The uniqueness is largely in the culture – how the people act, behave, are held accountable, and work with one another; how organizational arrangements are established and used; and how the organizational performance is evaluated relative to the external environment. There are, however, ubiquities. Among global leaders and organizations effective with planning, leading, and sustaining change, the use of measures and metrics is paramount. Just as the product development model disaggregates its work so too can an overall organization be disaggregated to recognize the need for change and to do so. Effective change agents and organizational change endeavors proactively manage organizational performance regarding all six dynamic components of the organization and the subcomponents of organizational arrangements and people.

Measuring Organizational Performance

Often change is associated with failure – a gap between actual performance and desired performance.[14] Effective change starts by proactively managing discrepancies and demands between expected targets and actual performance. Performance demands are derived from external and internal pressures. Internal pressures are those downward pressures originating from within the organization or upward pressures based on employee demands. Thus, internal pressures are those that address and react to internal processes and relationships. Conversely, external pressures stem from the organization's relationship with social, economic, and political environments. These external pressures include government regulation, culture, competition, and consumer behavior. Only when a discrepancy or demand is uncovered or forecasted to occur and change is deemed necessary does a planned change effort take place.

Certainly, failure or success is only determined if a performance goal is established and actively measured. Thus, the active use of performance measures – baselines, targets, data points, trend analyses – is a contributing factor to organizational change success. The reason for this is that when actively measuring performance, trends can be observed and action taken to address concerned areas of performance. Ideally, trends would be uncovered and addressed before a significant issue develops, which can lead to reaction, haste, or an unplanned set of activities.

If performance is not measured, the need for change may not be determined until a catastrophic error or a crisis occurs. This often results in the need for reactive change, which is extremely difficult to plan and lead due to the hurried nature associated with reaching an improved future-state. As noted in the opening chapter of this book, when we react, we do not calculate risk versus benefit adequately or thoroughly map a plan for action. Reactive change, rather than proactive change, often results in higher costs, longer schedules, and lower customer value and satisfaction.

As illustrated in Figure 7-1, the result of organizational performance is determined by the people in the organization. The skills, knowledge, and abilities of people coupled with the way in which they work in groups and teams and use technology is only part of the inner-workings of the organizational picture. The other part is the organizational arrangements. These arrangements include the structure, processes, practices, policies, reward mechanisms, decision-making protocols, mission, vision, and values upheld by people in the organization. Each of these elements associated with organizational dynamics can and should be measured with mission, vision, and values of the organizational arrangements being used to align business operations and program strategies, initiatives, goals, and objectives and all other sub-components of people.

Successful change is all about people. To effectively plan, lead, sustain, and adapt to change, organizational leaders and change agents must believe that employees are the differentiating asset in the organization. The idea that employees are the most valuable asset is more than a mere cliché within leading global organizations. From a leader's perspective this includes valuing the contributions of employees, being able to relate to people, and fostering relationships that are collaborative. Leaders of change trust people, their strengths, and their contribution, and understand that organizational change is effective only because the people involved in the change effort are effective. This is not to suggest there is no oversight or management. The grounding premise is performance. So, while there is trust, respect, and collaboration, there is a clear expectation that people matter and performance matters.

It is the people that not only provide the means for performance within the organization, but also the culture of the organization. Often, we are told by executives that "to succeed, I need to change our organizational culture." This is an inaccurate target for change, but perhaps a worthwhile by-product of human activity. It is not the culture that master change agents seek to change, but rather the way performance is measured and how people and organizational arrangements are established in whole that creates the culture of the organization. Culture will only change when aspect(s) of organizational arrangements and people components change. So, do not aim to change organizational culture – it will change when organizational arrangements and people change. And, to be effective, you cannot simply offer lip service to these issues.

An executive attempting to 'modernize' a geographically-distributed multi-use health facility noted this as he was leaving his position after peer executives and others merely offered lip service to the business transition effort associated with a significant organizational change endeavor:

> *"From my earliest time in this position it has seemed ironic to me that millions of dollars were being spent on experts in architecture, engineering and construction to design and build a new physical structure for the hospital but there was no plan to bring in experts to help build a new business structure and culture; the very heart of the operation of the hospital. This vital work of building a new business structure and culture for the organization was apparently expected to be carried out entirely by hospital staff who have no expertise in the disciplines necessary to make this process successful. What is more, the people at the hospital were apparently expected to do this while carrying on their usual daily work assignments. I saw this as a sure recipe for failure."*

He went on to explain what most frustrated change agents note: "There is a need for an integrated approach to change." Often senior executives spend an extraordinary amount of time attempting to perfect strategy, yet they spend very little time even thinking about the business transition needed for effective change. This point alone makes a significant difference between those expert with organizational change and the novice.

Sometimes the effectiveness in planning, leading, and sustaining change is immediately challenged because individuals within the firms resist the use of proactive and effective performance measures and metrics. Additionally, for those that struggle with successfully deploying change, we have found there is often a resistance to standards such as project methods, development procedures, and other protocols used and relied on heavily by consistently-successful organizations. Organizations that integrate and standardize disciplines such as project and program management, portfolio management, and business transition management as a comprehensive organizational change management strategy are most effective in planning, leading, and sustaining change.

Resistance to Change

The capacity for human change is prevalent. It seems, however, that while people can in fact change, it is their unwillingness to do so that needs to be addressed as a critical success factor in organizational change. The idea of change is often accompanied with fear due to uncertainty and perhaps denial, which manifests resistance. For most people, change is not easy and, therefore, change can be stressful. The response to change is a personal one based on experience and understanding. Individual resistance can be found in personal anxiety, which is the primary source of stress during times of change. Arnold Judson outlined six determinants of organizational resistance to change including feelings about the change, conflict between cultures and what is to be changed, the number of unanswered questions that arise during the change effort, historic events, the extent that the change threatens basic needs, and the extent that the change impacts self-worth.[15]

In addition to Judson's determinants, James O'Toole outlined thirty-three hypotheses for why change is resisted.[16] The psychological and social dynamics that contribute to resistance are vast. Short of revisiting O'Toole's complete list, four stand as paramount and need explanation. Kathy Milhauser, a seasoned veteran with a leading global apparel company recently conducted a detailed case study describing the importance of the instinctive response to change, the need to belong to a group, the power of identity, and the organizational mindset.[17] These four complement the findings from O'Toole and help explain why people resist change.

Instinctive response to change

People naturally resist anything that is outside of their control. The fight or flight response to an external threat is alive and well in our organizations. At the deepest level, individuals have a need for control of things that affect them. No one wants to be trapped, and most of us become quite illogical and emotional when we are backed into a corner. Change that is imposed on people can invoke quite violent resistance, purely due to the psychological affect of losing control.[18] Conversely, we are an inquisitive species and the grass is indeed always greener on the other side of the fence. So, change that is induced in an individual because they see that there is a better way to do things and that adapting their behavior is in their own best interests is quite natural. Therefore, change that is induced internally instead of imposed externally is bound to be met with less resistance and more buy-in due to the sense of ownership of the change.

The need to belong to a group

One of the most basic needs we have as human beings is the need to belong. We belong to a family, we belong to a culture, and we belong to groups that we associate with in our personal and professional lives. All of these associations participate in the formation and sustenance of our identity.[19] That identity creates a sense of security that tells us who we are and that we are not alone. This need for belonging can translate into extremely strong teams in the organizational workplace when identity is reinforced by being a member of the team where values are shared, mindsets about how things ought to be are strengthened, and individuals feel like they are part of something larger than themselves and that something they believe in.

The power of group identity

Groups form identities by creating boundaries between themselves and outsiders. In fact, one of the ways for a group to become clear on the behaviors that are acceptable for membership is to reinforce the behaviors that are unacceptable to the group.[20] Most of us have heard the phrase 'what this team needs is a common enemy' in the workplace. Threats to a group's identity and way of being are frequently galvanizing forces that bring teams together as if they were building a wall around their territory in an attempt to defend it. High performing teams have very clear rules for behavior and criteria for who is in and who is out of the team. Ask anyone who has joined a team and struggled to be accepted. It is not always clear what the rules are for how new members are meant to behave, but it often becomes very clear when one of those rules is broken. Boundaries form as groups strengthen their identity by reinforcing acceptable and unacceptable behaviors and creating clear distinctions between the behaviors of the in-group and those of the out-group. Change that threatens those boundaries will be resisted, often before it is even thoroughly examined. It is rarely the content of the change that is the problem. It is simply the fact that the change is being imposed from outside the group boundaries that creates the resistance.

The organizational mindset

Organizational mindsets are formed by the way things worked in the past. We have all heard the phrase, 'it has always been done this way'. Our natural response to the person saying this might be that they are just resistant to change. But why do they think this way? Why do 'old-timers', and sometimes even newer employees instinctively seem to know how things are supposed to be done, and fiercely guard against anything that threatens the 'it has always been done this way mindset? Could it be that the affect of cultural heritage inside organizations is more significant than most of us realize? Studies have shown that the behaviors of organizational founders and long-term executives often become legendary in the stories that are told for decades to follow.[21] These stories form mindsets that reinforce how a person is meant to behave in the organization. The old-timers in the organization have seen the change fads come and go. What has lasted has been the culture that they have increasingly learned to cling to, and in clinging to it they have strengthened and reinforced it. For the newer employees, these legends and stories become larger than life as they strive to make sense of how to be successful in the organization amid changing markets and external forces. These mindsets are hard to see and even harder to track to their source, but any anthropologist will tell you that the effect of tribal knowledge and oral history on a society is profound. Organizations are no different. Any change effort that threatens the perception of how things ought to be in the organization is bound to meet resistance.

Milhauser's four points are logical and provide a glimpse into what needs to be done to effectively build a readiness for change and successfully bring about organizational change. Specifically, since there is an instinctive response to change, successful change agents build stakeholder involvement with the change, thus building an understanding of the problem or opportunity and establishing a sense of ownership of the change among the stakeholders. In essence, the change agent serves as a guide rather than a director for the change.

As a guide, the effective change agent must establish a common purpose and sense of team in which everyone can belong. This does not suggest everyone gets along harmoniously all of the time, but rather there is a strong sense of mission, purpose, shared values, and common focus on results from which all stakeholders can hold one another accountable. Collectively, this accountability helps the team form an identity and over time this builds a strong culture. Most successful firms form that identity around the critical organizational change success factor of key performance measures because this creates a sense of continuous improvement based on external and internal metrics, which in itself is a change-ready mindset. This mindset exists in most high-performing teams that are industry innovators, global leaders, and trend setters.

Building a readiness for change within an organization does not end with addressing Milhauser's four points. The following section describes additional methods for overcoming resistance and building a readiness for change organization.

Overcoming Resistance and Building Readiness for Change

While change agents and organizational leaders can never eliminate resistance completely, effective organizational change does recognize the need to mitigate resistance, thus supporting the individual in coping with feelings of stress and progressing toward a readiness and adoption of the change. Again, here, firms effective at organizational change management see this as obvious, while most firms view this as costly, time consuming, and expendable. Perhaps Richard DeFrank and John Ivancevich captured it best in that "organizations that ignore the impact of stress on their employees and their productivity [especially in times of change] do so at their own peril."[22]

The single most effective tool used to overcome resistance and to build a readiness for change is communication. The information employees receive about a change and the means by which they receive it impacts their willingness to support and participate in the change. Thus, messaging and inclusion are important during times of organizational change. The types of messages abound when it comes to change. Depending on the timing (associated with the lifecycle of the project for change), messages must include the need for change, the ability to change, the valence for the change, the existing support for the change, and the appropriateness of the change. Other messages that increase the probability for effective change include the strategic reasoning for the change, the decision-making processes planned for change, and the methods, phases of work, and associated tasks of the change implementation plan.

These aspects of communication are all rather rational. Employees, however, are not fully rational beings, especially in times of change. While we can be rational, we are often irrational due to emotions, which influence behavior and actions, some of which can be unpredictable, making change difficult. Therefore, communication must address not only rational needs, but emotional needs and thought processes of the people involved.

Reasoning about organizational change through rational means can be done through the use of facts, figures, timelines, and measures as already noted. Communication to the emotional side of people takes on a different form and address Milhauser's work relative to group identity, belonging, and mindset. Beyond words, numbers, graphs, and rational analysis, effective change includes communication of corporate history, linking the past to the future in as linear a fashion as possible so as to draw a connection to where the company has been, where it is, and where it intends to be in the future. This is often accomplished through the use of sentimental stories that leverage abilities to overcome obstacles. Additionally, communication must align the change with not only strategy, but importantly, organizational values, beliefs, commitments, higher purpose of meaning of work and service (see Table 7-1). This type of communication includes self identity and heritage, and requires empathy and genuine concern for people. As such, the communication of change needs to address how the change benefits the organization, the employee, and other stakeholders – especially customers and the communities in which they work and live.

Rational Communication	Emotional Communication
Facts	History
Figures	Stories
Timelines	Values
Expectation	Purpose
Measures	Mission
Metrics	Service

Table 7-1: Rational versus emotional communication

It's About the People

As the statistics suggest, failure is often the case when it comes to change. It is important to note that most change endeavors do not fail because of some technical issue, but rather because of the human nature of the change. A new CEO of a global company recently tried to change strategic directions.[23] He tried to change the company with his intellect alone and without trying to move people emotionally. After a year of failed attempts, he was fired.

As we have already noted from Noel Tichy, the noted scholar and author, while managerial knowledge and skills in the areas of finance, manufacturing, and marketing are important for organizational success, they are woefully insufficient for effectively planning, leading, and sustaining organizational change. Effective organizational change is about . . .

- creating active involvement among stakeholders
- establishing teamwork, commitment, and accountability
- honesty, direct assertiveness, and collaborative challenging

- open dialogue and solutions-focused work efforts
- aligning purpose, mission, values, and personal activities to a larger goal
- a culture concerned with continued improvement

Beyond the understanding that people create the performance of the organization, successes at an individual level in times of change increase self-efficacy. Similarly, successes at a team and company level increase corporate-efficacy. This is the reason most recommendations about change include the notion of start small with little wins. Allowing little wins to build upon one another generates momentum and understanding about how organizations actually work – that is to say how individuals actually work within organizations. This reinforces the need to disaggregate large-scale change into smaller, more manageable and measurable changes.

It may seem as if organizational change management and business transition management is all about the soft skills. One study analyzed the results from implementing an enterprise-wide change across 150 distributed locations of a single company.[24] To study the organizational effect of the soft skill affect, some of the locations emphasized so-called soft(er) skills than others and the variances were analyzed based on total sales at points during and after change implementation. The findings indicated higher sales volumes in the locations where:

1. Top management presented the need and plan for change in person rather than via phone or video;

2. The change was incremented in stages rather than all at once;

3. Announcements and change activities were constant and in short intervals (every week) rather than

sporadic with longer lead times (3 to 4 or more weeks); and

4. Involvement of senior leaders, middle managers, and employees was prevalent as compared to the contrary.

The soft skills paid hard dividends. Not only did revenues increase in the locations where soft skills were employed, but it also affected morale. Often during times of change, the uncertainty and anxiety leads to increased in-fighting, decreased productivity, and attrition. The locations that realized increased revenues also realized increased morale and lower attrition rates as compared to the other locations. Soft skills help change mindsets and attitudes, long-standing and defunct corporate cultures, enliven commitment, and build a sense of team that motivates and encourages involved concern and participation. The bottom line is that, while organizational change is not all about soft skills, these skills do seem to provide the meaningful difference between organizational change success and failure.

Milhauser's research regarding resistance helps to make sense of organizational change failures. She went on to outline the role that senior leaders play in planning, leading, and sustaining organizational change success. The typical response to the problem of change resistance is to institute programs to convince people that the change being implemented is good. The irony of this approach is that the change management program itself becomes an external force that has the potential to invoke resistance response at the individual, group, and organizational level. It is essential to remember that anything that threatens individual or group identity by coming from outside is going to meet a natural resistance response. Whether the change is rationally clear for the better or not will be decided by the individuals and groups affected by the change. Change happens most effectively from the inside out.

So what can the senior leaders of an enterprise do to ensure a greater probability of success for their global transition change efforts? Learnings from Milhauser and global leading organizations suggest the following strategies:

1. Engage individuals in defining change;

2. Embed change agents inside teams;

3. Create externally-focused teams; and

4. Communicate an alignment with the organizational mindset.

Engage individuals in defining change

If imposing change on people creates a natural response of resistance, then it is only logical that we would engage those individuals in defining the change. For whatever reason, this is rarely done well in organizations. It is highly encouraged to involve stakeholders in the change. The enlightened change management team might interview some "end users" or "change targets" to see what their needs are, but they then typically go off to a conference room somewhere for weeks or even months to design the change effort based on that input. Even more enlightened change management teams will pull individuals out of their normal work setting to participate in the change effort, again going off to a conference room to design the change; but this time, taking representatives of the change target group along with them. This approach engages individuals as team members in defining change. But remember what we learned about group identity? There is a statute of limitations for how long a member can be gone from a group before they become part of the "out" group instead of the "in" group. They quickly become part of the external threat to the group, and no longer part of the team that will be affected by change.

Another approach is to design the change inside the target group instead of outside of it. Organizations involved in Lean process improvement efforts have an elegant way to lead change from the inside out following the Kaizen method. Kaizen, loosely translated from Japanese, stands for continuous improvement of an iterative nature. Groups pull out of the day-to-day work for a short period of time (hours or days) to document their process, identify common problems, and develop solutions. They then execute their change plan in an iterative fashion, reflecting on results and making adjustments in a structured fashion. This is typically an internally-focused effort aimed at process efficiency inside the group, but the same idea can be used to integrate external data that is creating the need for change. The role of the change agent in this scenario is that of facilitator, or guide as mentioned earlier, instead of influencer, or director, as the individual team members examine the triggers for change and define their response to those triggers under the guidance of a trained facilitator.

Embed change agents inside teams

One of the challenges to the approach of engaging individuals and teams in defining their own change is the skill gap. A group of individuals with the mission to build software or design products will not typically have training or experience in leading processes to facilitate change. The role of change agent becomes essential in guiding the team through this process, developing their skills and understanding, and ensuring that the change is well organized and facilitated using proven business transition and project management methods. But again, remember in-group and out-group behavior. If the change agent comes from outside of the group, they are once again part of that external force to which the group has formed resistance. The group may be passively polite and cooperative during the change workshop, but the change agent (and leadership sponsor) will generally be baffled a week or month later when they find out that the group is not implementing their own change plan. Why? Because the change agent was not part of the team.

Consider instead what happens when a change agent is embedded inside the team. They go through the process of adapting to group norms, defining an identity with the group, and developing a sense of urgency for why the team needs to change. They come to the change effort with change leadership skills and the external orientation that helps them see why change is needed. As they become part of the group, they develop a sense of belonging and understanding of group needs that helps them bridge the gap between the internal realities of the team and the external forces to which they need to adapt. This change agent, when accepted by the group as an "in-group" member, has a powerful ability to lead change from the inside.

Create externally-focused teams

Another strategy is to create externally-focused teams that understand what is needed to be successful inside their boundaries while keeping their eyes focused on the external landscape. This strategy works well in knowledge worker teams where expertise in processing information is relatively high; for example, in product development teams that are tuned-in to their consumer or customer needs. Recent trends in distributed teams may be making this even more critical as well as facilitating this external orientation. If a team has a strong group identity based on a shared understanding of why they exist, what they need to do to thrive, and what their boundaries for behavior are, they have the potential to bring significant insights from the external environment back to the team. Organizations that are doing this well have found these teams to be extraordinarily adaptable to change and quick to respond to opportunities

Communicate an alignment with the organizational mindset

Regardless of the approach chosen by organizational leaders: to engage employees in defining their own change, to embed change agents inside teams, or to create externally-focused teams, it continues to be essential that communication inside and across the change effort is aligned with the organizational mindset. Consider an organization that has been in place for many years and has cultural artifacts that communicate a solid, stable, and consistent approach to business based on openness, integrity, and honesty. How might this organization respond to a change campaign that tells them "the world is changing and we have to quickly adapt, be fluid and dynamic!" If the message is in conflict with the experiences of the past as well as the behaviors that have been rewarded and memorialized, it will be considered artificial and dishonest. On the other end of the spectrum is an organization that was founded by entrepreneurial behavior. Rules were meant to be broken, authority resisted, and irreverence justified. How might this organization respond to a change approach that is highly structured and includes detailed requirements and timelines for everything that needs to happen in the project plan? Clearly there would be a disconnect between the experience of being in this organization and the expectations of the change, which again comes across as dishonest and reinforces the belief that the change is a threat to not only the individual, but the integrity of the organization.

No amount of logic is going to convince individuals in either of these organizations to support the change. Furthermore, these approaches will taint the change effort with an air of dishonesty, distrust, and may lead to leader credibility issues and scapegoating. Change messages must be aligned to organizational realities; better yet, change messages should be communicated from inside out as individuals, groups, and the organization at large assess what needs to change, design their response, and communicate their success stories as contributions to the evolving organizational mindset.

Critical factors for change

The following offers a short list of critical factors for effective change.

- Organizations are dynamic due to six interrelated components including organizational arrangements, people, performance, external environment, continuous diagnosis and monitoring, and organizational culture and work unit climate. The influencing factors of change stem from diagnosing performance and the external environment from which change occurs with organizational arrangement and people. This process manifests the organization's culture.

- Change is often resisted. To mitigate this instinctive response, build a coalition with a sense of belonging, a clear and strong identity, and a change-ready mindset among the employees of the firm.

- Communication is the single most effective tool to overcome change resistance and build a readiness for change. Both rational and emotional communication tactics are needed to address resistance and build readiness.

- Additionally, readiness involves engaging individuals to define and initiate the change, embedding change agents inside the team yet working for the operations of the business, creating an externally-focused team, and constantly communicating.

- A framework for change is necessary for success. At a high level, change traverses a current state, through a transition state, to a future state. At a more detailed level, the change framework must incorporate project, program, and product lifecycle phases since it is through these means that change is planned, led, and sustained within organizations. The framework is a process in which once the future state is realized, performance measures and metrics are under constant diagnosis, seeking out the next need for change.

Looking Ahead

Transitioning an enterprise into a global competitor requires a significant amount of organizational change and an equally significant amount of time to complete the transition. This is due to the fact that organizations are complex entities, both in structure and in human behavior. Initiating change in any one area – for example flattening an organizational structure to accommodate effective global collaboration – causes change in other areas such as new roles and responsibilities for employees.

This interconnectivity of structure and behavior change is the primary reason why successful organizations use an incremental and methodical approach to global transition. In the final chapter, we introduce a simple framework and methodology for driving incremental organizational change.

CHAPTER EIGHT

A Global Transition Framework

"Knowing is not enough; we must apply. Willing is not enough; we must do."

- Goethe

As previously stated, execution of a globalization strategy requires a significant amount of organizational change in order to ensure effective execution in the new global environment. The scope of change, the sequencing of change activities, and the timing of change will be determined by the business goals driving the global strategy. For example, if an enterprise wishes to expand into new, emerging markets to achieve continued revenue growth, it may employ a globalization strategy to move portions of its product or service development to the targeted emerging markets to establish a local presence and employ local talent.

This globalization strategy will initiate a variety of organizational changes that will be necessary to ensure that future product and service development execution in a globally-distributed model will be successful in delivering the globalization business results intended. In this scenario, a new program-based development model may need to be deployed causing a change in both organizational and team structures, new roles and responsibilities for employees, new skills and competency may be required, new performance measures and rewards systems may need to be designed, and new cultural integration activities may have to be deployed. As one can see, the scope of change required can be significant and complicated due to the interdependencies between the elements undergoing change. However, until these organizational changes begin to take place, the global team leaders within an enterprise will have to battle an array of barriers and challenges while they try to effectively execute their global product and service development projects and programs.

To be fully successful, focused thought and energy must be expended to determine what needs to change, in what order, and over what duration to enable the global project and program teams to achieve the intended business results. This effectively creates a road map for change. With the road map in place, the organization can begin its incremental, methodical approach to global transition. To guide the transition, it is highly beneficial to utilize a consistent framework for transition change management.

A Framework for Implementing Change

There is a wealth of information available that tells us how difficult organizational change can be. What is missing in this information, however, is good detailed explanation on how best to actually implement the change – how to transition an organization from a current state to a future state. Peter Senge and his associates noted this challenge over a decade ago[1] as too did Michael Beer and Nitin Nohria as they noted that existing theory about organizational change is not sufficient to address the practical needs of business transition.[2] More recently, April Boyington Wall's dissertation work focused on the need for a practical organizational change process, technique, or formula available to plan, lead, and sustain change.[3]

Perhaps the two most prominent models used for organizational change today are John Kotter's eight-steps model and William Bridges' transition model.[4,5] In his book, Leading Change, Kotter outlines eight steps critical for effective change. The eight steps include: (1) establish sense of urgency, (2) form a guiding coalition, (3) create (shared) vision, (4) empower others to act on the vision, (5) plan and create short-term wins, (6) consolidate improvements, (7) produce more change, and (8) institutionalize new approaches. Part of the challenge of Kotter's model comes in his recommendation that these eight steps must be followed sequentially because, as he states, "skipping steps only creates the illusion of speed."[6] To be sure, the challenge is not in skipping steps so much as it is in the sequence. Change agents that we spoke with note no problem with the value of the eight steps, but indicate that, for instance, establishing a sense of urgency is an ongoing effort and is not accomplished prior to forming the coalition or empowering others. Rather, it is ongoing through the idea of creating and realizing short term wins. In all, the eight steps are fine to add to a list of success attributes, but offer little in the way of the details of planning, leading, and sustaining change.

Bridges' work consolidated change into three phases. He suggested there is an ending, a neutral zone, and the new beginning. This is a good starting point for organizational change. Identifying a high-level philosophy or stages of work is good for a mind frame. Three phases is what we recommend as well based on our practice and research. Interestingly, all change theories and philosophies of thought can be described as phases of work and most boil down to the originating thought on change – that of Kurt Lewin.[7]

To start building a framework for effective organizational change, a high-level view is necessary. All change essentially traverses three stages or phases: from a current state, through a transition state, to a future state. The current state, sometimes referred to as the AS-IS state, is associated with the identified need for change. The future state, sometimes referred to as the TO-BE state, is the desired state that can only be realized through a transition state from current to future. We use these terms because they are commonly used within product, project, and program management work, which as previously noted are the means to bring about change. This approach to change requires an integrated framework for change that incorporates not only the needed elements of business transition, but also the elements of project management. The individuals and teams we have worked with have designed an integrated model that utilizes a phased framework approach. Figure 8-1 illustrates the high-level phases of change associated with project management phases of work.

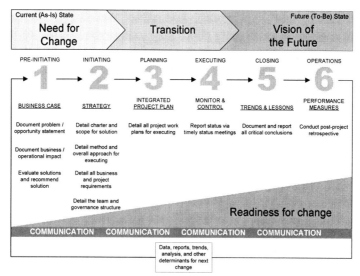

Figure 8-1: An integrated framework for organizational change

The essence of change management strategy is the transition between two states – a current state in which a determined need for change occurs and the future state wherein the vision of the new, desired organization resides. However, the current state phase and future state phase are equally important because that is where "the business" identifies the need and operationalizes the new state. One of the reasons most change endeavors fail is due to poor management between the phases – the hand-offs between the business and transition project managers and their teams.

The following outlines the important activities within each phase of the framework. An important component to keep in mind as you read through the details of this model is that performance is the driver as diagnosed through internal measures and the pressures of the external environment.

Pre-Initiating Phase

The focus in the pre-initiating phase is to detail a business case. What is the business rationale for the change? Can the change be directly supported by improvements anticipated to the business? Who are the key stakeholders? It is important to keep in mind that the business case is critical, but it should be detailed to the extent necessary. Therefore, while a major company merger or acquisition likely has a thick and intense case for consideration, a software upgrade across national borders should be less dramatic. Nevertheless, successful change endeavors all have a clearly-documented, easy-to-understand, rational business case. Essentially, this case validates the need for change and should do so based on performance needs and is supported by a cost/benefit analysis, resource needs, a risk and complexity assessment, and the organization's readiness to address the change. Once the business case is approved, the work activities matriculate to the initiating phase.

Initiating Phase

The focus during initiating is to leverage the detail in the business case to detail a change strategy. The strategy keeps the business case "alive" by further detailing it and moving it closer to action. Specifically, the strategy serves to detail the rules of engagement for the change endeavor. It reinforces not only the need for change, but also details the team, structure, requirements, best practices to follow, scope, and charter of the change. Moreover, this is the time that the team – both executives and project-level staff – defines what success is and how it will be obtained. Important here is the team approach to initiating the change. Those change agents who seek and gain involvement here will reap the benefits in future phases of work.

This phase details how the change endeavor will be planned and led, and should provide answers to the following questions:

- How will the project team involve and leverage other personnel and stakeholders without interruption to current operations?

- What are the critical skills needed on the team and who are the key leaders of the endeavor?

- How will the intended change be managed?

- How will the change project and business measures and metrics be monitored and reported against baselines and toward targets?

- What are the success criteria?

- How will the team know when the intended change is successfully completed?

- What are the generalized steps or approach planned for the change?

- Will it be administered through pilot tests and short-terms wins (recommended) or a broad-based implementation across the enterprise?

- What are the implications to competing projects and resources?

- What decision model will be used throughout the change?

Once the questions are answered in the form of a change strategy, and the strategy is approved, the work activities matriculate to the planning phase.

Planning Phase

The focus during planning is to build a functional and realistic integrated project plan. At this point, the core project leadership team is fully engaged and dedicated to the change success. The team (likely led by the program manager, project managers, and business transition manager) is responsible for detailing individual plans for the change (such as technology, training, resistance management, communication, implementation, gap analysis, and so on) and integrating them wholly and completely. Meaning the plans are detailed to the point of understanding dependencies and interdependencies for work tasks and personnel. As such, this is a comprehensive plan aimed to address the rationale in the business case and reflects the business, technical, and personnel change requirements for success as needed based on the gap between the current state and future state. It will include planned actions, a schedule, resources, funding, risk mitigation, metrics, training, structural changes, and the documentation needed to support the change.

Executing Phase

This phase of work focuses on the execution of the integrated plan according to its schedule, monitoring and controlling the actual activities relative to the plan, and making adjustments as needed to deliver business success. Monitoring and controlling is essential for successful projects. Providing status updates to the project team, committees, and other stakeholders is necessary, especially as this work aims at summarizing critical aspects of the project work (accomplishments over a specified period of time and the upcoming work efforts) from which awareness can be gained and planning and decision-making can be conducted.

Also, during this phase, stakeholder awareness of the need for change, their skills to make the required changes, their commitment to putting changes into place, and the overall coordination of the entire change endeavor are determined. There are a number of times throughout a project change endeavor when a readiness assessment should be conducted to (1) establish a baseline; (2) validate the effectiveness of the communication plan and employee awareness, involvement, and preparedness based on the execution of core and facilitating work plans; and (3) assess risks and plan necessary mitigations to go live with the changes. Each time readiness is assessed, it yields findings for what leaders need to do to intervene for greater readiness. Figure 8-2 graphically illustrates the reciprocating process of the work plans, communications, and readiness relative to go live.

Figure 8-2: Interrelatedness of work plans based on communication and readiness

Closing Phase

In this phase there is a transfer of ownership that occurs from the project transition team to the business operations. This is a point where the business case and performance measures are re-emphasized. It is critical that the transfer here and the work between this closing phase and the operations phase not be neglected. Sometimes transition project teams and project leaders have a tendency to dissolve the team too quickly, jeopardizing the effectiveness of the project solution. More, not less, communication and coordination is needed during and between these last two phases of work. The transition project or program leader "owns" the solution until the business operation's owner assumes control, as determined by success factors detailed in the business case.

Most projects capture lessons learned through means of a post action review. We have already mentioned the need for retrospectives throughout the project and change endeavor. Specifically, in this phase of work the aim of such work is to learn and improve personnel, project, program, and organization efficiency and effectiveness. To continuously improve requires investigation into successes and failures. Trends and lessons learned documentation should be gathered from all stakeholders and based on an open system concept. Once gathered and vetted, the lessons must be (widely) shared for organizational performance improvement.

Operations

The active use of performance measures and metrics is a contributing factor to organizational success. Data associated with key performance indicators are the means for decision making and determination of major transition projects. As such, the performance measures continue in importance here because they serve to quantify critical aspects of the business and determine (as noted in Figure 8-1) the next need for change. For greatest effectiveness, performance measures should be clearly defined, used consistently, and should be accompanied by measurement baselines and targets. Additionally, keep in mind that these operational measures should be diagnosed relative to the external (market) environment.

In practice, the global transition change framework should be used for all organizational factors that may be involved in implementing a firm's globalization strategy. To summarize many of the key points addressed throughout this book, the following factors within an organization may have to undergo change in order to positively affect the environment in which a global project or program team leader operates as a firm transitions itself from a domestic to global business:

- Organizational and team structures that expand collaborative team dynamics;

- The blending of cultural components (country, company, and functional) to enable global communication and collaboration;

- A development model that supports the interdependent nature of global product and service development activities;

- New skills and competencies for global project and program managers;

- Training and development programs for global employee skill development and cultural awareness;

- Performance measures, metrics, and rewards and recognitions that support global development success ahead of functional and individual success;

- Communication and collaboration technologies that enable a distributed workforce; and

- Commonality in methods, processes, and tools use across the organization.

Additionally, more tactical factors may be required such as consolidation of employee services and support into centralized locations, and changes to the supply chain. All transition change efforts, whether strategic or tactical, will benefit from the use of a transition framework to guide activities.

Turning the Corner at Keytron

It has been nearly three years since the day Scott Jones realized that the company that he was working for was a globalization follower in the consumer electronics industry. Today, however, he is more upbeat about Keytron's prospects of one day becoming a leading global company within the industry. This is because he has seen significant progress toward the alignment of the firm's global execution abilities to their globalization strategy. In fact, performance measures such as on-time delivery and increased market share in emerging markets continue to improve business quarter by quarter.

According to Jones: "I have learned many things about global product development but one of the key lessons is that it takes time and considerable effort to begin to realize your globalization goals." To their credit, Jones and Keytron at large have made significant progress in their globalization journey. "When I look back, I can see we've made some significant changes," explains Jones. "Our development organization is now more collaborative since we removed many layers with the organizational structure, the adoption of a program-based development model has been well received, our employees are more aware and embracing of our cultural differences, and we're beginning to introduce common development process and tools across the company to increase global team efficiency."

Keyron's latest global transition change program involved the implementation of an enterprise level electronic collaboration space and data repository tool. "We're getting much better at implementing our organizational change projects and development of new products," stated Jones. "This is mainly due to the addition of Deborah Wayne who is a transition change management expert." Wayne has been put in charge of managing the major global transition programs initiated at Keytron.

Wayne is a veteran program manager with her fair share of failures and successes – more consistent successes now having learned from her failures in the past. A significant learning from past failures is the need for change management strategies integrated into her program and project plans to assure success. When Wayne first started working at Keytron, she heard comments from senior executives such as the following: "Effective change management is a critical need for the success of our projects and our company;" "The organization really needs to spend quality time focusing on change management;" "We need more details on change management plans and business transition planning;" and "We need to understand the 'how-to' of change management execution."

To begin with, Wayne spent a considerable amount of time teaching and coaching the executives and senior leaders at Keytron what was missing from their teams and project protocols and how the missing ingredients – an organizational change management framework and business transition management skills – were leading to the company's high transition change failure rate. Knowing this directly impacted financial standings, customer satisfaction, and employee moral, they listened.

Scott Jones' program office morphed into a "global process center of excellence" so as to shed the myopic label and attention solely from program management to a more effective solutions center for the organization including not only program management, but also enterprise portfolio management, measures and metrics support, and business transition expertise. Additionally, the transition program teams are now being appropriately staffed, according to Wayne, with change agents and business transition managers knowledgeable in the business and who are functional as team players working for the global program managers. Wayne found herself in need of these folks as she took on her latest challenge – instituting the new electronic collaboration system for the firm's global program teams.

In addition to introducing new technology to improve global team performance, Wayne understood the implication this had with organizational arrangements and people (see figure 7-1). A change in one warrants investigation as to how the rest of the system may change. A simple change in technology could have extreme implications with the rest of the components associated with people and many, perhaps all, of the organizational arrangement components. Additionally, the change would certainly have impact on performance and therefore be known from diagnosis and comparative analysis with external forces such as competitors. All of this change would shape the organization's culture and work unit climate.

Navigating the Transition Framework

Wayne noted, "The first thing to consider when getting assigned to a project like this is the business case. Do I understand the full business case, in all of its complexity? If so, I can then adequately staff the project." It is important with complex projects such as this that impact distributed sites, core technology, business process, and human behavior, that the team leaders have support from the business executives. Not just buy-in, but active support. The first test of the level of senior management support comes in the pre-initiating phase of the transition change framework.

"Further, with an understanding of the business case, I was able to adequately plan the appropriate method, strategy, and tactics to deliver the program." Wayne points out that there is delineation between the business case and strategy. This delineation is noted in Figure 8-1 by the phases of Pre-Initiating and Initiating. The reason for the delineation is one of portfolio planning. Often projects leap from ideation to execution. A more planned approach assures project alignment relative to organizational goals and resource constraints. Summarizing a business case for decision purposes prior to building a strategy starts a dialogue about the project and limits the resources involved. Many times, this serves to break down the amount of work in between decision points.

Once the business case and strategy were approved, Wayne negotiated the use of two committees for the program as she entered the planning phase of the framework. According to Wayne, "The first was an executive steering committee that helped me overcome budgetary and personnel constraints and barriers based on the program needs. I connected with this group regularly early in the program and then monthly for status briefs and risk-mitigation discussions. The second was an operational leadership committee comprised of the key managers who have operational duties impacted by the change. The operations committee helped me to overcome tactical challenges associated with business processes and program needs. I connected with this group much more often than with the executives, weekly during some parts of the program."

Wayne's transition team helped her focus on the organizational change details of the program. "Just as I had technical teams work the details of networks, databases, user interfaces, and the like, I relied heavily on a business transition team to support the planned application of change throughout the company." Wayne noted the need to have a human resources manager involved in the project tangentially for support due to the fact that job duties were modified, which warranted revised job descriptions. Figure 8-3 diagrams the collaboration space transition program organization structure.

An interesting component of Wayne's team was the use of a communications officer. It was clear that a good communication plan was vital for program success. In the complexity of most programs today, a communication officer is needed to help support the rest of the business transition activities and the program manager. Choosing a "point person" or transition leader

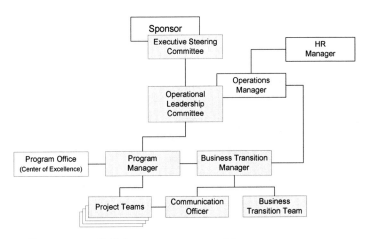

Figure 8-3: Collaboration space transition program structure

in the business unit to act as a liaison between the program's business transition team and the business unit workers in every country was vital for effective communication. Additionally, this liaison helped build involvement among stakeholders, which led to acceptance and enthusiasm for the change.

"One of the most challenging aspects of a program like this," noted Wayne "is aligning readiness of all aspects of the organization that is changing. There was the technology component involving hardware, software, networking, data integration, and associated training of staff. There were business process changes and associated training of staff. There was change in employee skill requirements and role definition and, finally, changes in operational and performance measures and metrics." To manage all of this, Wayne conducted a readiness assessment periodically throughout the execution phase of the transition change framework.

Readiness for change assessments determined stakeholder awareness of the need for change, their skill to make the required changes, and their commitment to putting changes into place. According to Wayne, "We tracked detailed components in five areas including resources, education and training, awareness and communication, organizational dynamics, and implementation planning."

- **Resources:** This category assesses the physical, financial, and personnel resources needed for the change initiative and time allocation.

- **Education and Training:** This category assesses personnel development needs typically associated with education or training relative to the change.

- **Awareness and Communication:** This category assesses the communication and involvement from the perspective of building awareness for the change.

- **Organizational Dynamics:** This category assesses all the dimensions and dynamics of organizations (organizational arrangements and people).

- **Implementation Planning:** This category assesses the business case, strategy, and integrated plan(s) associated with implementing the change program.

Using a readiness assessment tool is important on all change programs. This tool helps to determine effectiveness of the program team, their work involving people from the business units in the change, the effectiveness of the communication plan and other facilitating plans, and the reality of the program's scheduled timeline.

The critical challenge with programs such as the one Wayne was leading is creating and sustaining momentum. This is why so many change models and theories call for planning short-term wins. "It is important" notes Wayne, "that there be deliverables or releases in short time lapses. At least every couple months a major deliverable or release is needed. Under this scenario, every week would likely require major tasks to be complete leading up to the release. It is important to realize the interdependencies of work, especially when working across geographies. So, I required a fully integrated plan and schedule and had, minimally, weekly team meetings that were open to everyone on the program, If necessary, I held multiple meetings and video recorded them to make them available across time zones. I often travelled and hosted the status meetings in different locations throughout the program. This seemed to help build team cohesion and involvement."

A bit more discussion is warranted about Wayne's integrated plan and schedule. With a program this complex, there are multiple schedules. The technology team has design and development schedules. The test team has a schedule linked to the technology schedule. The trainers have curriculum to design and use relative to a training schedule, which must be linked to the technology schedule. Additionally, this curriculum must be aligned with a business process, practice, and policy change for which there is another schedule. Conducting the readiness assessments is associated with resistance management planning and has its own schedule. It was Wayne's role to integrate all of these schedules.

She began this process by creating a detailed program map of cross-project deliverables (see Chapter Four). "The program map helped me to plan and track deliverables, but perhaps even more important than that, it helped me plan resources. It is vitally important for communication purposes to know and be able to explain why, when, and how organizational resources will be used. Having worked on both local and global projects, this is exponentially more important on a global scale," says Wayne.

According to Wayne's business partners, she was successful in deploying the global collaboration system into the organization. Although the program was delivered three months late, based on a two-year plan, the delay was due to information captured during the readiness assessment indicating that the alignment of all necessary change elements was not ready, warranting a three-month delay.

According to Scott Jones, there were three critical results from this program. "First, there were efficiencies gained as measured by cost, quality, financial, and operational determinants. Second, there was effectiveness gained as measured by employee satisfaction and collaboration output. Third, and perhaps most important, there is perceived survivability achieved as measured by the organization's capacity for more change that is inevitably on the horizon." Although a bit late, Wayne's collaboration space organizational change endeavor was successful and she has already been deployed to Keytron's next global transition change program.

Final Thoughts on Leading Global Teams

Plenty of debate exists on whether the pace of globalization being experienced today is sustainable, or whether globalization trends will eventually reverse and we will see companies begin to pull their operations back to their home countries. Whether globalization is sustainable or irreversible is probably something that only time will tell. Certainly, the world has become an interdependent place at a magnitude never experienced in history. The continued intertwining of national economies toward the creation of a single world economy, along with continued creation of new communication and collaboration technologies serves to support the assertion that globalization is irreversible. However, as the people of previous centuries realized, the wildcards in this game are political ideologies and policies. Empowerment of anti-globalization fundamentalists has the potential once again to move the globalization forces in a direction that breaks the current global interdependencies.

Regardless, for the foreseeable decades ahead, global market expansion and establishing competitive advantage will continue to be significant strategies for companies. The companies that can learn to adapt to this complex environment and compete successfully will be the survivors and industry leaders of the future. This means that there will be no shortage of demand and opportunity for those individuals who are adept at leading global project and program teams. Unfortunately, it will also mean that there will be no shortage of global execution barriers and challenges facing our globally-expanding companies.

The material contained within this book is built upon two key points that are a direct result of our research on the practices of leading global companies. First, the senior leaders within an organization must step up and become directly involved in ensuring that their global project and program team leaders are set up for success in executing the firm's globalization strategy.

It is insufficient for senior executives to focus solely on setting the globalization strategy. They also must stay personally involved in removing the organizational and environmental barriers that prevent successful global product and service development execution. Specifically, this involves creating a horizontally-structured organization that facilitates global collaboration, adopting a development model that effectively aligns global execution with globalization strategies, investing in cultural growth and awareness as well as global team leader development, and personally championing all major global transition change endeavors.

Second, global project team leaders must realize that their success is more dependent upon good leadership skills, techniques, and competency rather than core project management abilities. Upon this realization, they must focus their skills and career development toward obtaining and successfully utilizing leadership abilities in a global team environment.

This goes well beyond learning techniques such as managing time zone differences or becoming proficient in using collaboration and communication tools for distributed teams. Rather, it means becoming an expert in human behavior in a global environment. Success in leading a global team is less dependent upon one's ability to assign tasks to people or to integrate a set of functional schedules, and more dependent upon one's ability to influence a group of people with widely-varying backgrounds to act and perform as a cohesive team focused on a common purpose and mission.

Success in leading global projects is therefore a matter of establishing a strong partnership between an organization's senior managers and global team leaders to ensure that the globalization strategy and global execution are tightly aligned and supportive of one another.

References

Chapter 1

1   Friedman, Thomas L. *The World is Flat*. New York: Farrar, Straus and Giroux Publishing, 2006.

2   Cohen, Ed. *Leadership Withut Borders: Successful Strategies from World-class Leaders*. Hoboken, NJ: John Wiley & Sons (Asia), 2007.

3   Steger, Manfred B. *Globalization: A Very Short Introduction*. London, England: Oxford University Press, 2003.

4   Smith, A. *An inquiry into the nature and causes of the wealth of nations*. New York: The Modern Library, 1776/1994.

5   Bootle, R. "We now face Keynesian conditions and need truly Keynesian solutions." *London Telegraph*. 2008. <http://www.telegraph.co.uk>

6   World Bank official website. <http://www.worldbank.org>.

7   World Trade Organization website. <http://www.gatt.org>.

8   Steger, Manfred B. *Globalization: A Very Short Introduction*. London, England: Oxford University Press, 2003.

9   Steger, Manfred B. *Globalization: A Very Short Introduction.* London, England: Oxford University Press, 2003.

10 Friedman, Thomas L. *The World is Flat.* New York, NY: Farrar, Straus and Giroux Publishing, 2006.

11 American Productivity and Quality Center. "Improving Collaboration for Product and Service Development." *Final Report APQC: 2008.* 2008.

12 Anonymous. "Global Product Development (GDP) – Moving from Strategy to Execution." *Business Week.* Business Week Research Services, 2006.

Chapter 2

1   Anonymous. "Global Product Development (GDP) – Moving from Strategy to Execution." *Business Week.* BusinessWeek Research Services, 2006.

2   Ibid.

3   Hesslebein, Frances, Marshall Goldsmith, and Iain Somerville. *Leading Beyond the Walls: How High-performing Organizations Collaborate for Shared Success.* San Francisco, CA: Jossey-Bass Publishing, 1999.

4   Cohen, Ed. *Leadership Without Borders: Successful Strategies from World-class Leaders.* Hoboken, NJ: John Wiley & Sons (Asia), 2007.

5   Duarte, Deborah L. and Nancy Tennant Snyder. *Mastering Virtual Teams: Strategies, Tools, and Techniques That Succeed.* San Francisco, CA: Jossey-Bass Publishing, 2001.

6   Hesslebein, Frances, Marshall Goldsmith, and Iain Somerville. *Leading Beyond the Walls: How High-performing Organizations Collaborate for Shared Success.* San Francisco, CA: Jossey-Bass Publishing, 1999.

[7] Adler, Nancy J. *From Boston to Beijing: Managing with a World View.* Cincinnati, OH: South Western, 2002.

[8] Duarte, Deborah L. and Nancy Tennant Snyder. *Mastering Virtual Teams: Strategies, Tools, and Techniques That Succeed.* San Francisco, CA: Jossey-Bass Publishing, 2001.

[9] Milosevic, Dragan Z., R.J. Martinelli, and J.M. Waddell. *Program Management for Improved Business Results.* Hoboken, NJ: John Wiley & Sons, 2007.

[10] Duarte, Deborah L. and Nancy Tennant Snyder. *Mastering Virtual Teams: Strategies, Tools, and Techniques That Succeed.* San Francisco, CA: Jossey-Bass Publishing, 2001.

[11] Al-Ani, Ban, Keith Edwards, and Erik Simmons. *Distributed System Development: An Empirical Pilot Study of Current Practices.* 2007.

[12] <http://www.worldtimezone.com>.

[13] Milosevic, Dragan Z., R.J. Martinelli, and J.M. Waddell. *Program Management for Improved Business Results.* Hoboken, NJ: John Wiley & Sons, 2007.

Chapter 3

[1] American Productivity and Quality Center. "Improving Collaboration for Product and Service Development." *Final Report, APQC.* 2008.

[2] Duarte, Deborah L. and Nancy Tennant Snyder. *Mastering Virtual Teams: Strategies, Tools, and Techniques That Succeed.* San Francisco, CA: Jossey-Bass Publishing, 2001.

[3] Pearce, J. II and R. Robinson, Jr. *Strategic Management: Formulation, Implementation, and Control.* New York, NY. McGraw-Hill Publishing, 2000,

[4] Milosevic, Dragan Z., R.J. Martinelli, and J.M. Waddell. *Program Management for Improved Business Results*. Hoboken, NJ: John Wiley & Sons, 2007.

[5] American Productivity and Quality Center. "Improving Collaboration for Product and Service Development." *Final Report, APQC: 2008.* 2008.

[6] Hesslebein, Frances, Marshall Goldsmith, and Iain Somerville. *Leading Beyond the Walls: How High-performing Organizations Collaborate for Shared Success.* San Francisco, CA: Jossey-Bass Publishing, 1999.

[7] Anonymous. "Global Product Development (GDP) – Moving from Strategy to Execution." *Business Week.* Business Week Research Services. 2006

[8] American Productivity and Quality Center. "Improving Collaboration for Product and Service Development." *Final Report: APQC: 2008.*

[9] Stevens, Richard. *Systems Engineering: Coping with Complexity.* Great Britain: Pearson Education, 1998.

[10] Martinelli, R., and Waddell, J. "Program Management: Linking Business Strategy to Product and IT Development." *Project Management World Today.* September-October 2003.

[11] Friedman, Thomas L. *The World is Flat.* New York: Farrar, Straus and Giroux Publishing, 2006.

[12] Milosevic, Dragan Z., R.J. Martinelli, and J.M. Waddell. *Program Management for Improved Business Results,* Hoboken, NJ: John Wiley & Sons, 2007.

[13] American Productivity and Quality Center. "Improving Collaboration for Product and Service Development." *Final Report, APQC: 2008.*

14   Martinelli, Russ and Jim Waddell. "Demystifying Program Management: Linking Business Strategy to Product Development." *PDMA Visions Magazine.* January 2004.: pp 20-23.

15   McGrath, Michael E., Anthony, Michael T., and Shapiro, Amram R. *Product Development: Success Through Product and Cycle-time Excellence.* Stoneham, Ma: Butterworth-Heinemann Publishers, 1992.

16   Gladwell, Malcolm. *Outliers: The Story of Success.* New York, NY: Little, Brown and Company, 2008.

17   Kouzes, James M. and Barry Z. Posner. *The Leadership Challenge.* San Francisco, CA: Jossey-Bass, 2002.

18   American Productivity and Quality Center. "Improving Collaboration for Product and Service Development." *Final Report, APQC: 2008. 2008.*

Chapter 4

1   Lewis, James P. *Fundamentals of Project Management.* New York: AMACOM, 1997.

2   <http://www.globalprojectstrategy.com/lessons/airbus.html>.

3   <http://www.globalprojectstrategy.com/success_casestudy.html>.

4   Milosevic, Dragan Z., R.J. Martinelli, J.M. Waddell, *Program Management for Improved Business Results.* Hoboken, NJ: John Wiley & Sons, 2007.

5   Maxwell, John C. *The 21 Irrefutable Laws of Leadership.* Nashville, TN: Thomas Nelson Publishers, 1998.

6   Meyer, Marc H. and Alvin P. Lehnerd. *The Power of Product Platforms.* New York: Free Press Publishers, 1997.

7 Snyder, Bill. "Teams That Span Time Zones Face New Work Rules". *Stanford Business Magazine,* May 2003.

8 Milosevic, Dragan Z., R.J. Martinelli, J.M. Waddell. *Program Management for Improved Business Results,* Hoboken, NJ: John Wiley & Sons, 2007.

9 Cohen, Ed. *Leadership Without Borders: Successful Strategies from World-class Leaders.* Hoboken, NJ:John Wiley & Sons (Asia), 2007.

10 NASA Website: <http://nssdc.gsfc.nasa.gov/database/MasterCatalog?sc=1998-073A>

11 Al-Ani, Ban, Keith Edwards, and Erik Simmons. "Distributed System Development: An Empirical Pilot Study of Current Practices." 2007.

12 Gibson, Cristina B. and Susan G. Cohen. *Virtual Teams that Work.* San Francisco, CA: Jossey-Bass, 2003.

13 Holahan, Pat, Ann Mooney, Roger Mayer and Laura Finnerty-Paul. "Do Debates Get More Heated in Cyberspace? Team Conflict In The Virtual Environment." Howe School Alliance For Technology Management, Fall 2008.

14 Milosevic, Dragan Z., R.J. Martinelli, J.M. Waddell. Program *Management for Improved Business Results.* Hoboken, NJ: John Wiley & Sons, 2007.

15 Gibson, Cristina B. and Susan G. Cohen. *Virtual Teams that Work.* San Francisco, CA: Jossey-Bass, 2003.

16 Milosevic, Dragan Z., R.J. Martinelli, J.M. Waddell. *Program Management for Improved Business Results.* Hoboken, NJ: John Wiley & Sons, 2007.

17 Cohen, Dennis J. *The Project Manager's MBA.* San Francisco, CA: Jossey-Bass, 1994, 2001.

Chapter 5

[1] Gibson, Cristina B. and Susan G. Cohen. *Virtual Teams that Work*. San Francisco, CA: Jossey-Bass, 2003.

[2] Duarte, Deborah L. and Nancy Tennant Snyder. *Mastering Virtual Teams: Strategies, Tools, and Techniques That Succeed.* San Francisco, CA: Jossey-Bass, 2001.

[3] Anonymous. "Global Product Development (GDP) – Moving from Strategy to Execution." *Business Week*. BusinessWeek Research Services, 2006.

[4] <http://www.wiki.answers.com>.

[5] Lavell, D. and Russ Martinelli. "Program and Project Retrospectives: An Introduction." *PM World Today*, Volume X, Issue I, January 2008.

[6] Hofstede, G. *Culture's Consequences*. Beverly Hills, CA: Sage, 1980.

[7] Myers, David G. *Social Psychology*, 7th Edition. New York: McGraw-Hill, 2002.

[8] Jovanovic, J. and Candice Dreves. "Math, Science and Girls: Can We Close the Gender Gap?" National Network for Child Care, May 1996.

[9] House, Robert J. "How Cultural Factors Affect Leadership." *Knowledge@Wharton*, July 1999.

[10] Cannon-Bowers, J.A., Salas, E. "Reflections on Shared Cognition." *Journal of Organizational Behavior,* 195-202, 2001.

[11] Jetter, A. and Jose Campos. "Improving Collaboration in Multi-Ethnic Teams." *Program Management Forum*, 2008.

[12] Lawler, E.E., Mohrman, S.A., and Benson, G.S. *Organizing for High Performance: The CEO Report on Employee Involvement, TQM, Reengineering, and Knowledge Management in Fortune 100 Companies.* San Francisco: Jossey-Bass, 2001.

[13] Duarte, Deborah L. and Nancy Tennant Snyder. *Mastering Virtual Teams: Strategies, Tools, and Techniques That Succeed.* San Francisco, CA: Jossey-Bass, 2001.

[14] Qauppe, Stephanie and Cantafore Giovanna. "What Is Cultural Awareness, Anyway? How DO I Build It?". <http://culturosity.com>, 2005.

[15] Rynes, S.L., and Gerhart, B. *Compensation in Organization.* San Francisco, Jossey-Bass, 2000.

[16] Katzenbach, Jon R.., and Douglas K. Smith. *The Wisdom of Teams.* New York: Mckinsey & Company, 1999.

Chapter 6

[1] Cohen, Dennis J., Robert Graham, and Robert J. Graham. *The Project Manager's MBA.* San Francisco, CA: Jossey-Bass Publishing, 2001.

[2] Dupree, Max. *Leadership is an Art.* New York: Doubleday, 2004.

[3] Maxwell, John C. *The 21 Irrefutable Laws of Leadership.* Nashville, TN: Thomas Nelson, 1998.

[4] Pink, Daniel. *A Whole New Mind,* New York: Berkeley Publishing Co, 2006.

[5] Senge, Peter. *The Fifth Discipline,* New York: Doubleday, 1990.

[6] Keogh, J., Shtub, A., Bard, J.F., Globerson, S. *Project Planning and Implementation.* Needham Heights, Ma:Pearson Custom Publishing, 2000.

[7] Martinelli, Russ and Jim Waddell. "Power, Politics, and Program Management." *PMWorld Today,* Vol IV, Issue IV, April 2007.

8 Milosevic, Dragan Z., R.J. Martinelli, J.M. Waddell. *Program Management for Improved Business Results*. Hoboken, NJ: John Wiley & Sons, 2007.

9 Adler, Nancy J. *From Boston to Beijing: Managing with a World View*. Cincinnati, OH: South Western, 2002.

10 Ibid

11 Duarte, Deborah L. and Nancy Tennant Snyder. *Mastering Virtual Teams*. San Francisco, CA: Jossey-Bass, 1999.

12 Ibid

13 Pink, Daniel. *A Whole New Mind*. New York: Berkeley Publishing Co, 2006.

14 Adler, Nancy J. *From Boston to Beijing: Managing with a World View*. Cincinnati, OH: South Western, 2002.

15 Cherniss, Cary. "Business Case For Emotional Intelligence", 1999

16 Goleman, Daniel. *Emotional Intelligence: Why It Can Matter More Than IQ*. New York: Bantam Dell, 1995.

17 Bradberry, Travis and Jean Greaves. *The Emotional Intelligence Quick Book,* New York: Simon & Schuster, 2005.

18 Kutz, Mathew R'. "Contextual Intelligence: An Emerging Competency for Global Leaders." *Regent Global Business Review,* Regent University, August 2008.

19 Ibid

20 Milosevic, Dragan Z., R.J. Martinelli, J.M. Waddell. *Program Management for Improved Business Results*. Hoboken, NJ: John Wiley & Sons, 2007.

21 Gladwell, Malcom. *Outlier*. New York: Hachette Book Group Inc, 2008.

[22] Kolb, David. Experiential Learnings: Experience as the Source of Learning and Development, 1984.

[23] Queich, John A. and Helen Bloom. "Ten Steps To a Global Human Resources Strategy"

Chapter 7

[1] Toffler, A. *Future shock.* New York: Random House, 1970.

[2] Burke, W. W. *Organizational change: Theory and practice.* Thousand Oaks, CA: Sage, 2002.

[3] Conner, D. R. *Managing at the speed of change: How resilient managers succeed and prosper where others fail.* New York: Villard, 1992.

[4] Kotter, J. P. *Leading change.* Boston, MA: Harvard Business School Press, 1996.

[5] Cascio, W. F. "Whether industrial and organizational psychology in a changing world of work." *American Psychologist,* 50(1), 928-939, 1995.

[6] Vaill, P. *Learning as a way of being.* San Francisco, CA: Jossey-Bass, 1996,

[7] Drucker, P. F. "The coming of the new organization." *Harvard Business Review,* 66, 45-53, 1998.

[8] Cairncross, F. *The death of distance: How the communications revolution will change our lives.* Boston, MA: Harvard Business School Press, 1997.

[9] Colteryahn, K., & Davis, P. "Trends you need to know now." *Training & Development,* 50(1), 28-36, 2004.

[10] Machiavelli, N. *The Prince.* Herfordshire, Wordsworth Editions Limited, 1997.

[11] Kotter, 1990; Hammer and Champny,. 1993.

[12] Anonymous. "Global Product Development (GDP) – Moving from Strategy to Execution." *Business Week*. BusinessWeek Research Services, 2006.

[13] Bennis, W. G. *Changing organizations.* New York: McGraw-Hill, 1996.

[14] Weick, K. E., & Quinn, R. E. "Organizational change and development." *Annual Review of Psychology,* 50, 361-386, 1999.

[15] Judson, A. S. *Changing behavior in organizations: Minimizing resistance to change.* Cambridge, MA: Blackwell, 1991.

[16] O'Tool, J. *Leading change: The argument for values-based leadership.* New York: Ballantine Books, 1995.

[17] Milhauser, K. Unpublished case study. 2010

[18] Lewin, K. "Group decision and social change." *Readings in social psychology,* 330-344, 1947.

[19] Tajfel, H. *Human groups and social categories.* Cambridge, UK: Cambridge University Press, 1981.

[20] Tajfel, H., & Turner, J. C. (Eds.). *The social identity theory of intergroup behavior.* Chicago: Nelson-Hall, 1986.

[21] Hofstede, G., Neuijen, B., Ohayv, D. D., & Sanders, G. "Measuring organizational cultures: A qualitative/quantitative study across twenty cases." *Administrative Science Quarterly,* 35, 286-316. 1990.

[22] DeFrank, R. S., & Ivancevich, J. M. "Stress on the job: An executive update." *Academy of Management Executive*, 12(3), 55-66, 1998.

[23] Goleman, D., Boyatzis, R. and McKee, A. *Primal Leadership – Realizing the Power of Emotional Intelligence.* Boston, MA: Harvard Business School Press, 2002.

[24] Longbotham, G. J., & Longbotham, C. R. "A scientific approach to implementing change." *Journal of Practical Consulting*, 1(1), 19-24, 2006.

Chapter 8

[1] Jaworski, J., Gozdz, K., & Senge, P. "Setting the field: Creating the conditions for profound institutional change." Cambridge, MA: MIT Center for Organizational Learning, 1998.

[2] Beer, M., & Nohria, N. "Cracking the code of change." *Harvard Business Review*, 78(3), 133–141, 2000.

[3] Wall, A. B. (2004). "Mapping shifts in consciousness: Using a constructive developmental perspective to explore key variables in organizational transformation." Unpublished dissertation. Union Institute & University.

[4] Kotter, J. P. *Leading change.* Boston, MA: Harvard Business School Press. 1996.

[5] Bridges, W. *Managing transitions: Making the most of change.* Reading, MA: Addison-Wesley, 1991,

[6] Kotter, J. P. *John P. Kotter on what leaders really do.* Boston, MA: Harvard Business Press, 1999.

About the Authors

Russ Martinelli, senior program manager at Intel Corporation, has many years of experience leading global product development teams in both the aerospace and computing industries. Russ is also a co-founder of the Program Management Academy (www.programmanagement-academy.com), and co-author of the first comprehensive book on program management titled *Program Management for Improved Business Results.*

Tim Rahschulte is responsible for international management and leadership studies at George Fox University in Oregon. Additionally, he consults with state governments on matters of organizational change as a business transition architect and is an executive director at the Program Management Academy.

Jim Waddell, former director of program management for Tektronix, is currently an independent management consultant in his fields of expertise: program management and mergers and acquisitions. He has held a wide spectrum of management positions, has been a speaker at numerous conferences, and is a co-author of Program Management for Improved Business Results. Jim is also a co-founder of the Program Management Academy (www.programmanagement-academy.com).

Did you like this book?

If you enjoyed this book, you will find more interesting books at

www.MMPubs.com

Please take the time to let us know how you liked this book. Even short reviews of 2-3 sentences can be helpful and may be used in our marketing materials. If you take the time to post a review for this book on Amazon.com, let us know when the review is posted and you will receive a free audiobook or ebook from our catalog. Simply email the link to the review once it is live on Amazon.com, with your name, and your mailing address—send the email to orders@mmpubs. com with the subject line "Book Review Posted on Amazon."

If you have questions about this book, our customer loyalty program, or our review rewards program, please contact us at info@mmpubs.com.

ACROSS THE HALL
AROUND THE WORLD
TEAMBUILDING TIPS FOR DISTRIBUTED BUSINESSES

CLAIRE SOOKMAN AND SUSAN GARMS

Across the Hall, Around the World: Teambuilding Tips for Distributed Businesses

Having trouble engaging and energizing teams across your business? Many people are struggling with motivating teams, especially ones where some team members work in different locations -- even across the world.

In this book, Claire Sookman and Susan Garms, experts on motivating distributed (a.k.a. "virtual") teams, bring you a number of teambuilding activities and exercises that you can put to immediate use.

The techniques and exercises in this book will help you

- Build collaboration
- Help team members get to know each other
- Conduct more effective meetings
- Bridge the gap between different cultures, and
- Overcome the obstacles of working in virtual teams

ISBN: 9781554890606 (paperback)

Available from Amazon.com or your nearest book retailer. Or, order direct at www.MMPubs.com.

Tips for Virtual Team Management: Using the DiSC Behavioural Profile to Better Manage Distributed Teams

Is your team spread across the hall, the building, the city, the province or the state, the country, or even the globe? Guess what, you have a virtual team, Congratulations!

Now what? Well, as you know, creating virtual teams is not challenge-free.

The foundation of a strong virtual team is communication. But how do you get to know your team when you are not face to face? How do you know whether your team members are highly analytical or, at the other extreme, very social? And how do you figure it out with only virtual cues?

If you knew that, than you would know how to best communicate with them. This book will guide you through a step-by-step approach to identifying and adapting to the people on our team whether you are face to face or using email, instant messaging, teleconferences, or web-conferences.

With the help of this book, you can create a strong, cohesive virtual team that meets its objectives.

ISBN: 9781895186055 (Adobe PDF on CD-ROM)

Available from Amazon.com or your nearest book retailer. Or, order direct at www.MMPubs.com.

Flexible Project Management for Product Development

Traditional project management approaches are not sufficient for product development due to the complexity of getting a new product to market. Technology changes, personnel turnover, changing customer requirements, multi-site development, and unclear schedules are but a few of the variables that render conventional project management deficient.

Flexible Project Management for Product Development is a unique, downloadable, and fully-interactive electronic guide to allow you and your team to manage your development project in the middle of the turmoil created by global competition. This ebook is an Adobe PDF document that has been designed to be fully interactive; beyond just reading very useful material, you will be able to use the templates and tools and also be able to share the information with your peers around the world.

The material in this book has been field-tested by the authors and by many companies similar to yours. This is not a theoretical book that assumes "best-case-scenarios", which rarely happen in the real world of product development; rather, it equips you to deal with the ever-changing environment of product development particularly when you face a multi-site development project.

ISBN: 9781554890477 (Adobe PDF eBook)

Available from www.MMPubs.com.

Debriefs and Postmortems for Product Development

This downloadable and interactive guide allows your product team to use and apply "lessons learned" in an effective manner. Studies show that "postmortems" are the best way to improve the productivity of teams, better than training, books, seminars and other tools.

The ability to methodically identify areas of improvement from development programs and immediately apply them to upcoming efforts will result in improved productivity, more enthusiastic teams, and improved morale in your development organization.

This ebook was developed by veteran product development experts who know how to "trim" methods to their very essence to make them work, even in tumultuous environments where change is the rule of the day. It will guide you step-by-step, including all the forms, templates and specially process maps required. It will also help you to avoid the common mistakes many organizations make that block them from obtaining the full benefits from debriefs. Finally, it will show you how to prioritize improvement changes, and how to deploy them through the organization in a way that it is embraced by all.

ISBN: 9781554890507 (Adobe PDF eBook)

Available from www.MMPubs.com.

LaVergne, TN USA
08 April 2010
178607LV00002B/5/P